IRISH FIRESIDE FOLKTALES

Irish Fireside Folktales

by PATRICK KENNEDY

EDITED AND SELECTED BY
KARIN VON DER SCHULENBURG

THE MERCIER PRESS

DUBLIN and CORK

© This edition and selection The Mercier Press, 1969
Reprinted 1976

ISBN 0 85342 096 3

EDITOR'S NOTE AND ACKNOWLEDGEMENT

The present volume contains a selection of household stories taken from *The Legendary Fictions of the Irish Celts,* published by Macmillan in 1866, and from *The Fireside Stories of Ireland,* published by McGlashan and Gill in 1870. Forthcoming volumes will include stories of fairies, witches, and saints, ossianic and other tales.

I would refer any reader who wants to know more of Patrick Kennedy to James Delaney's admirable essay (*The Past,* No. 7, 1964).

Cover design: Inge Bourke

Based on a photograph by Colman Doyle

Reprinted Photo-Litho in the Republic of Ireland

CONTENTS

INTRODUCTION 7

I. JACK AND HIS COMRADES . . 11

II. THE BAD STEPMOTHER . . 19

III. ADVENTURES OF GILLA NA CHRECK
AN GOUR 25

IV. JACK THE MASTER AND JACK THE
SERVANT 34

V. I'LL BE WISER NEXT TIME . . 43

VI. THE THREE CROWNS . . . 46

VII. THE CORPSE WATCHERS . . 59

VIII. THE BROWN BEAR OF NORWAY . 63

IX. THE GOBAN SAOR . . . 74

X. THE GRATEFUL BEASTS . . 80

XI. THE LAZY BEAUTY AND HER AUNTS . 85

XII. HAIRY ROUCHY . . . 91

XIII. THE WISE MEN OF GOTHAM . . 100

XIV. THE GREEK PRINCESS AND THE YOUNG
GARDENER 104

XV. SHAN AN OMADHAN AND HIS MASTER 116

XVI. THE WONDERFUL CAKE . . . 125

GLOSSARY 127

INTRODUCTION

The fireside stories of the Irish people are part of a heritage unparalleled in the oral literature of the world. Certainly no other nation has preserved by word of mouth such an exuberance of riddles, sayings, curses, blessings, prayers and ballads. Nowhere has the art of storytelling been more richly developed than in Ireland; through the centuries generations of storytellers have handed down folktales of all kinds. At a time when modern life had not yet spread into the remotest corners of the countryside, storytelling was a favourite pastime and entertainment in the quietness and monotony of long country evenings. The voices of *seanchaí*, and wise woman, of wandering pedlar or spalpeen gathered the people round the fireside and audiences listened to legends and anecdotes, to religious, heroic and romantic tales. Through the voice of the storyteller the audience entered into the unseen world of the imagination; the world of magic and marvel, kings and queens, giants and gnomes, witches and fairies, warriors and saints: the world where time and place submit to the rule of fancy.

Many international tales have found their way into Ireland. Such stories as "Jack and his Comrades" or "The bad Stepmother" are told in many countries. Through the centuries they have been heard at a thousand Irish firesides. (It is interesting to see that Irish folklore offers hundreds of variants of one such international tale, against a few continental variants.) Blended, filtered and re-created through an Irish idiom and imagery, they emerge as unmistakably Irish in flavour and content.

7

Most stories in this book are of this international kind. They were written down by Patrick Kennedy, a Dublin bookseller, who might be regarded as one of the pioneers of folklore collecting. He was born in 1801 in Kilmishal, a small village in north-west County Wexford, and he lived the first twenty years of his life in the Mount Leinster range. A peasant himself, he grew up among the peasantry, went to the local school, became an elementary schoolteacher and later taught at the Kildare Place training school. By 1841 he had set up a little bookshop in Anglesea Street, Dublin, which seems to have been a meeting place for many booklovers and folklore enthusiasts. A contributor to various magazines, a friend and correspondent of many of his great literary contemporaries, he was highly respected and popular in his own day. When he died the leading newspapers praised him unanimously. They remembered him as a writer and literary critic, but above all as the folklorist who had bequeathed in his writing a record of Irish country life before the famine, "more faithful and more minute than Lord Devon's Commission or any other Blue Books". And from the many tributes there emerges the figure of a man who was full of modesty, charity, deep religious feeling and love of country.

In his writing he embodied oral lore, customs and beliefs as they had been current during his Wexford youth, between 1801 and 1821. "Do not you and I and others still retain many traditions of our native place?" he wrote in 1851 to the editor of the *Wexford Independent*. "In the present transition state of our country they are likely to be

8

lost and will it not be doing some service to preserve them however imperfectly?" He feared, he was " haunted by the horrid thought ", that through the effects of famine, emigration, literacy and the decline of the Irish language the whole wealth of Irish oral tradition might soon be lost, irrecoverably lost. In his *Legends of Mount Leinster* (1855), *The Banks of the Boro* (1867), *Evenings in the Duffrey* (1869), he presented Wexford ways and tales against a background of fiction. His other works, with the exception of a book of Irish anecdotes and a novel written under his pen-name Harry Whitney, are collections of traditional tales: *The Legendary Fictions of the Irish Celts* (1866), *The Bardic Stories of Ireland* (1871), and *The Fireside Stories of the Irish People* (1870).

Patrick Kennedy was born into an age when an awakening interest in folklore and folk literature was well under way. It was the great age of discovering and collecting the oral literature of the people. Though in his writing he limited himself to the traditions of Wexford, his reading went far beyond the boundaries of provincialism, extending to almost every collection then available. He deeply admired the famous collections by the Brothers Grimm, the Norwegian tales by Asbjornsen and Campbell's translation of Scottish-Gaelic tales. In his running comments and notes he referred to the Magyar, Polish, Russian, Hindoostan tales (most of which had appeared in German translation) and he liked to link his Wexford tales to those of other countries.

Patrick Kennedy knew that he was working " in the barren fields of a semi-English country " and that a much richer vein of material was to be found in the Irish-speaking areas. He humbly limited himself to what had been living tradition during the years of his Wexford youth. Fifty years after he heard his stories by some fireside, in some kitchen, he wrote them down as he remembered them. His sources were the people of Wexford: Mrs. K., " a woman of gentle manners who could recite passages from the *Iliad* and the greater part of the battle of Aughrim "; Jemmy Reddy, " gardener, horseboy, ploughman "; Owen Jourdan, " the hereditary faggot cutter ".

These years were a period of language transition. Stories that had been told in Irish for centuries were being told for the first time in English, a language only recently acquired. Not surprisingly, they still bear the mark of the Irish idiom. The turn of a phrase may prove to be a literal translation from the Irish, the structure of the sentence follows an Irish pattern. Irish words, quite naturally, appear in the flow of the English narrative. In their love of description, their submission to a formal pattern, these simple tales mirror many elements of the ancient art of story-telling. They are colourful, vivid, whimsical. Their attraction lies in their liveliness, in the use of narrative and dialogue, and of brief, sometimes moralising commentary. Everything is told as if it happened to the storyteller himself and as if these extraordinary events could happen to you or anybody.

The Mercier Press   Karin von der Schulenburg
Cork   April 1969
10

Jack and His Comrades

Once there was a poor widow, and often there was, and she had one son. A very scarce summer came, and they didn't know how they'd live till the new potatoes would be fit for eating. So Jack said to his mother one evening: " Mother, bake my cake, and kill my cock, till I go seek my fortune; and if I meet it, never fear but I'll soon be back to share it with you." So she did as he asked her, and he set off at break of day on his journey. His mother came along with him to the bawn gate, and says she,—" Jack, which would you rather have, half the cake and half the cock with my blessing, or the whole of 'em with my curse?" "O musha, mother," says Jack, "why do you ask me that question? Sure you know I wouldn't have your curse and Damer's estate along with it." "Well, then, Jack," says she, " here's the whole lot of 'em, and my thousand blessings along with them." So she stood on the bawn ditch and blessed as far as her eyes could see him.

Well, he went along and along till he was tired, and ne'er a farmer's house he went into wanted a boy. At last his road led by the side of a bog, and there was a poor ass up to his shoulders near a big bunch of grass he was striving to come at. "Ah, then, Jack asthore," says he, " help me out or I'll be drownded." " Never say't twice," says Jack, and he pitched in big stones and scraws into the

11

slob, till the ass got good ground under him. "Thank you, Jack," says he, when he was out on the hard road; "I'll do as much for you another time. Where are you going?" "Faith, I'm going to seek my fortune till harvest comes in, God bless it!" "If you like," says the ass, "I'll go along with you; who knows what luck we may have!" "With all my heart; it's getting late, let us be jogging."

Well, they were going through a village, and a whole army of *gorsoons* were hunting a poor dog with a kettle tied to his tail. He ran up to Jack for protection, and the ass let such a roar out of him, that the little thieves took to their heels as if the old boy was after them. "More power to you, Jack!" says the dog. "I'm much obliged to you: where is the beast and yourself going?" "We're going to seek our fortune till the harvest comes in." "And wouldn't I be proud to go with you!" says the dog, "and get shut of them ill-conducted boys; purshuin to 'em!" "Well, well, throw your tail over your arm and come along."

They got outside the town, and sat down under an old wall, and Jack pulled out his bread and meat, and shared with the dog; and the ass made his dinner on a bunch of thistles. While they were eating and chatting, what should come by but a poor half-starved cat, and the moll-row he gave out of him would make your heart ache. "You look as if you saw the tops of nine houses since breakfast," says Jack; "here's a bone and something on it." "May your child never know a hungry belly!" says Tom; "it's myself that's in need of your kindness. May I be so bold as to ask

12

where yez are all going?" " We're going to seek our fortune till the harvest comes in, and you may join us if you like." "And that I'll do with a heart and a half," says the cat, " and thankee for asking me."

Off they set again, and just as the shadows of the trees were three times as long as themselves, they heard a great crackling in a field inside the road, and out over the ditch jumped a fox with a fine black cock in his mouth. " Oh, you anointed villain!" says the ass, roaring like thunder. " At him, good dog!" says Jack, and the word wasn't out of his mouth when Coley was in full sweep after the *Moddhera Rua*. Reynard dropped his prize like a hot potato, and was off like a shot, and the poor cock came back fluttering and trembling to Jack and his comrades. " O musha, neighbours!" says he, " wasn't it the height o' luck that threw you in my way! Maybe I won't remember your kindness if ever I find you in hardship; and where in the world are you all going?" " We're going to seek our fortune till the harvest comes in; you may join our party if you like, and sit on Neddy's crupper when your legs and wings are tired."

Well, the march began again, and just as the sun was gone down they looked around, and there was neither cabin nor farmhouse in sight. " Well, well," says Jack, " the worse luck now the better another time, and it's only a summer night after all. We'll go into the wood, and make our bed on the long grass." No sooner said than done. Jack stretched himself on a bunch of dry grass, the ass lay near him, the dog and cat lay in the ass's warm lap, and the cock went to roost in the next tree.

13

Well, the soundness of deep sleep was over them all, when the cock took a notion of crowing. "Bother you, *Cuileach Dhu*!" says the ass: you disturbed me from as nice a wisp of hay as ever I tasted. What's the matter?" "It's daybreak that's the matter: don't you see light yonder?" "I see a light indeed," says Jack, "but it's from a candle it's coming, and not from the sun. As you have roused us we may as well go over and ask for lodging." So they all shook themselves and went on through grass, and rocks, and briars, till they got down into a hollow, and there was a light coming through the shadow, and along with it came singing, and laughing, and cursing. "Easy, boys!" says Jack; "walk on your tippy toes till we see what sort of people we have to deal with." So they crept near the window, and there they saw six robbers inside, with pistols, and blunder-bushes, and cutlashes, sitting at a table, eating roast beef and pork, and drinking mulled beer, and wine, and whisky punch.

"Wasn't that a fine haul we made at the Lord of Dunlavin's!" says one ugly-looking thief with his mouth full, "and it's little we'd get only for the honest porter: here's his purty health!" "The porter's purty health!" cried out every one of them, and Jack bent his fingers at his comrades. "Close your ranks, my men," says he in a whisper, "and let every one mind the word of command." So the ass put his fore-hoofs on the sill of the window, the dog got on the ass's head, the cat got on the dog's head, and the cock on the cat's head. Then Jack made a sign, and they all sung out like mad.

"Hee-haw, hee-haw!" roared the ass; "bow-wow!" barked the dog; "meaw-meaw!" cried the cat; "cock-a-doodle-doo!" crowed the cock. "Level your pistols!" cried Jack, "and make smithereens of 'em. Don't leave a mother's son of 'em alive; present, fire!" With that they gave another halloo, and smashed every pane in the window. The robbers were frightened out of their lives. They blew out the candles, threw down the table and skelped out at the back door as if they were in earnest, and never drew rein till they were in the very heart of the wood.

Jack and his party got into the room, closed the shutters, lighted the candles, and ate and drank till hunger and thirst were gone. Then they lay down to rest;—Jack in the bed, the ass in the stable, the dog on the door mat, the cat by the fire, and the cock on the perch.

At first the robbers were very glad to find themselves safe in the thick wood, but they soon began to get vexed. "This damp grass is very different from our warm room," says one; "I was obliged to drop a fine pig's crubeen," says another; "I didn't get a spoonful of my last tumbler," says another; "and all the Lord of Dunlavin's gold and silver that we left behind!" says the last. "I think I'll venture back," says the captain, "and see if we can recover anything." "That's a good boy!" said they all, and off he went.

The lights were all out, and so he groped his way to the fire, and there the cat flew in his face, and tore him with teeth and claws. He let a roar out of him, and made for the room door, to look for a candle inside. He trod on the dog's tail, and if he did, he got marks of his teeth in his arms, and legs, and thighs. "Millia murdher!" cried he; " I wish I was out of this unlucky house." When he got to the street door, the cock dropped down upon him with his claws and bill, and what the cat and dog done to him was only a bite to what he got from the cock. " Oh, tattheration to you all, you unfeeling vagabones!" says he, when he recovered his breath; and he staggered and spun round and round till he reeled into the stable, back foremost, but the ass received him with a kick on the broadest of his small clothes, and laid him comfortably on the dunghill. When he came to himself, he scratched his head, and began to think what happened him; and as soon as he found that his legs were able to carry him, he crawled away, dragging one foot after another, till he reached the wood.

"Well, well," cried they all, when he came within hearing, " any chance of our property?" "You may say chance," says he, " and it's itself is the poor chance all out. Ah, will any of you pull a bed of dry grass for me? All the sticking plaster in Enniscorthy will be too little for the cuts and bruises I have on me. Ah, if you only knew what I have gone through for you! When I got to the kitchen fire, looking for a sod of lighted turf, what should be there but a *colliach* carding flax, and you may see the marks she left on my face with the cards. I made to the room door as fast as I could, and who should I stumble over but a cobbler and his seat, and if he did not work at me with his awls and his pinchers you may call me a rogue. Well, I got away from him somehow, but when I was passing through the door, it must be

the divel himself that pounced down on me with
his claws, and his teeth, that were equal to six-
penny nails, and his wings—ill luck be in his road!
Well, at last I reached the stable, and there, by
way of salute, I got a pelt from a sledge-hammer
that sent me half a mile off. If you don't believe
me, you can go and judge for yourselves." " Oh,
my poor captain," says they, " we believe you to
the nines. Catch us, indeed, going within a hen's
race of that unlucky cabin!"

Well, before the sun shook his doublet next
morning, Jack and his comrades were up and
about. They made a hearty breakfast on what was
left the night before, and then they all set off to
the castle of the Lord of Dunlavin, and gave back
all his gold and silver. Jack put it all in the two
ends of a sack, and laid it across Neddy's back, and
all took the road in their hands. Away they went,
through bogs, up hills, down dales, and sometimes
along the yalla high road, till they came to the hall
door of the Lord of Dunlavin, and who should be
there, airing his powdered head, his white stockings, and his red breeches, but the thief of a porter.

He gave a cross look to the visitors, and says he
to Jack, " What do you want here, my fine fellow?
there isn't room for you all." " We want," says
Jack, " what I'm sure you haven't to give us—and
that is, common civility." " Come, be off, you lazy
geochachs!" says he, " while a cat 'ud be licking
her ear, or I'll let the dogs at you." " Would you
tell us," says the cock that was perched on the
ass's head, " who was it that opened the door for
the robbers the other night?" Ah! maybe the
porter's red face didn't turn the colour of his frill,

and the Lord of Dunlavin and his pretty daughter, that were standing at the parlour window unknownst to the porter, put out their heads. " I'd be glad, Barney,". says the master, " to hear your answer to the gentleman with the red comb on him." " Ah, my lord don't believe the rascal; sure I didn't open the door to the six robbers." " And how did you know there were six, you poor innocent?" said the lord. " Never mind, sir," says Jack, " all your gold and silver is there in that sack, and I don't think you will begrudge us our supper and bed after our long march from the wood of Athsalach." " Begrudge, indeed! Not one of you will ever see a poor day if I can help it."

So all were welcomed to their heart's content, and the ass, and the dog, and the cock got the best posts in the farmyard, and the cat took possession of the kitchen. The lord took Jack in hand, dressed him from top to toe in broadcloth, and frills as white as snow, and turnpumps, and put a watch in his fob. When they sat down to dinner, the lady of the house said Jack had the air of a born gentleman about him, and the lord said he'd make him his stewart. Jack brought his mother, and settled her comfortably near the castle, and all were as happy as you please. The old woman that told me the story said Jack and the young lady were married; but if they were, I hope he spent two or three years getting the education of a gentleman. I don't think that a country boy would feel comfortable, striving to find discourse for a wellbred young lady, the length of a summer's day, even if he had the *Academy of Compliments* and the *Complete Letter Writer* by heart.

The Bad Stepmother

Once there was a king, and he had two fine children, a girl and a boy; but he married again after their mother died, and a very wicked woman she was that he put over them. One day when he was out hunting, the stepmother came where the daughter was sitting all alone, with a cup of poison in one hand and a dagger in the other, and made her swear that she would never tell any one that ever was christened what she would see her doing. The poor young girl took the oath, and just after the queen took the king's favourite dog and killed him before her eyes.

When the king came back, and saw his pet lying dead in the hall, he flew into passion, and asked who done it; and says the queen, " Who done it but your favourite daughter? There she is—let her deny it if she can." The poor child burst out a-crying, but wasn't able to say anything in her own defence because of her oath. Well, the king did not know what to do or to say. He cursed and swore a little, and hardly ate any supper. The next day he was out a-hunting the queen killed his little son, and left him standing on his head on the window-seat of the lobby.

Well, whatever way the king was in before, he went mad now in earnest. " Who done this?" says he to the queen. " Who but your pet daughter?" " Take the vile creature," says he to two of his footmen, " into the wood, and cut off her two hands at the wrists, and maybe that'll teach her not to commit any more murders. Oh, Vuya, Vuya!" says he, stamping his foot on the boarded floor, " what a misfortunate king I am to lose my childher this way, and had only the two. Bring me back the two hands, or your own will be off before the sun is down."

When he stamped on the floor a splinter ran up into his foot through the sole of his boot; he didn't mind it at first, he was in such grief and anger. But when he was taking off his boots, he found the splinter fastening one of them on his foot. He was very hardset to get it off, and was obliged to send for a surgeon to get the splinter out of the flesh; but the more he cut and probed, the further it went in. So he was obliged to lie on a sofa all day, and keep it poulticed with bowl almanac or some other plaster.

Well, the poor princess, when her hands were cut off, thought the life would leave her: but she knew there was a holy well in the wood, and to it she made her way. She put her poor arms into the moss that was growing over it and the blood stopped flowing, and she was eased of the pain, and then she washed herself as well as she could. She fell asleep by the well, and the spirit of her mother appeared to her in a dream, and told her to be good, and never forget to say her prayers night and morning, and she would escape every snare that would be laid for her.

When she awoke next morning she washed herself again, and said her prayers. She heard a noise, and she was so afraid that she got into a low broad tree that hung over the well. And who did she see but a girl with a piece of bread and butter in one hand, and a pitcher in the other, coming and stooping over the well. She looked down through the branches, and if she did, the girl saw her face in the water, and thought it was her own. She looked at it again and again, and then without waiting to eat her bread or fill her pitcher, she ran back to the kitchen of a young king's palace that was just at the edge of the wood. " Where's the water?" says the housekeeper. " Water!" says she; " it'ud be a purty business for such a handsome girl as I grew since yesterday, to be fetchin' water for the likes of the people that's here. It's married to the young prince I ought to be." " Oh! to Halifax with you," says the house-keeper. " I'll soon cure your impedence." So she locked her up in the store-room, an' kep' her on bread and butter.

To make a long story short, two other girls were sent to the well, and all came back with the same story. An' there was such a *thravally* ruz in the kitchen about it at last, that the young king came to hear the rights of it. The last girl told him what happened to herself, and nothing would do the prince but go to the well to see about it. When he came he stooped and saw the shadow of the beautiful face; but he had sense enough to look up, and he found the princess in the tree.

Well, it would take me too long to tell yez all the fine things he said to her, and how modestly she answered him, and how he handed her down, and was almost ready to cry when he saw her poor arms. She would not tell him who she was, nor the way she was persecuted on account of her

21

oath; but the short and the long of it was, that he took her home, and couldn't live if she didn't marry him. Well, married they were; and in course of time they had a fine little boy; but the strangest thing of all was that the young queen begged her husband not to have the child christened till he'd be after coming home from the war that the King of Ireland had just then with the Danes.

He agreed, and set off to the camp, and just as his foot was in the stirrup he gave a beautiful jewel to her. Well, he wrote to her every second day, and she wrote to him every second day, and dickens a letter ever came to the hands of him or her. For the wicked stepmother had her watched all along, and such a bribe she gave to the postman that she got all the letters herself. Well, the poor king didn't know whether he was standing on his head or his feet, and the poor queen was crying all day long.

At last there was a letter delivered to the king; and this was wrote by the wicked stepmother herself, as if it was from the young queen to one of the officers, asking him to get a furlough, and come and meet her at the well in the forest. He got this officer, that was as innocent as the child unborn, put in irons, and sent two of his soldiers to put the queen to death, and bring him his young child safe. But the night before, the spirit of the queen's mother appeared to her in a dream, and told her the danger was coming. " Go," said she, " with your child to-morrow morning to the well, and dress yourself in your maid's clothes before you leave the house; wash your arms in the well once more, and take a bottle of the water with you, and return to your father's palace. Nobody will know you. The water will cure him of the disorder he has, and I need not say any more."

Just as the young queen was told, just so she done; and when she was after washing her face and arms, lo and behold! her nice soft hands were restored; but her face that was as white as cream was now as brown as a berry. So she fell on her knees and said her prayers, and then she filled her bottle, and set out for her father's court with her child in her arms. The sentries at the palace let her pass when she said she was coming to cure the king; and she got to where he was lying in pain before the stepmother knew anything about it, for herself was sick at the time.

Before the princess opened her mouth the king loved her, she looked so like his former queen and his lost daughter, though her face was so swarthy. She hardly washed his wound with the water of the holy well when out came the splinter, and he was as strong on his limbs as a new ditch.

Well, hadn't he great *cooramuch* about the brown-faced woman and her child, and nothing that the wicked queen could do would alter his opinion of her. The old rogue didn't know who she was; but it was her nature to be jealous of every one that the king cared for.

In two or three weeks the war was over, and the young king was returning home, and the road he took brought him by his father-in-law's. The old king would not let him pass by without giving him an entertainment for all his bravery against the Danes, and there was great huzzaing and cheering as he was riding up the avenue and through the courtyard. Just as he was alighting, his wife held up his little son to him, with the jewel in his little hand.

He got a wonderful fright. He knew his wife's features, but they were so tawny, and her pretty brown hands were to the good, and the child was his own picture, but still she couldn't be his false princess. He kissed the child, and passed on, but hardly said a word till dinner was over. Then says he to the old king, " Would you allow a brown woman and her child that I saw in the palace yard, to be sent for, till I speak to her?" " I will, indeed," said the other; " I owe my life to her." So she came in, and the young king made her sit down very close to him. " Young woman," says he, " I have a particular reason for asking you who you are, and who is the father of that child." " I can't tell you that, sir," said she, " because of an oath I was obliged to take never to tell my story to any one that was christened. But my little boy was never christened, and to him I'll tell everything. My little son, you must know that my wicked stepmother killed my father's favourite dog, and killed my own little brother, and made me swear never to tell any one that ever received baptism, about it. She got my own father to have my hands chopped off, and I'd die only I washed them in the holy well in the forest. A king's son made me his wife, and she got him by forged letters to send orders to have me killed. The spirit of my mother watched over me; my hands were restored; my father's wound was healed; and now I place you in your own father's arms. Now, you may be

24

baptized, thank God! and that's the story I had to tell you."

She took a wet towel, and wiped her face, and she became as white and red as she was the day of her marriage. She had like to be hurt with her husband and her father pulling her from each other; and such laughing and crying never was heard before or since. If the wicked stepmother didn't make her escape, she was torn between wild horses; and if they all didn't live happy after— that you and I may!

Adventures of Gilla na Chreck an Gour

Long ago, a poor widow lived down near the iron forge, by Enniscorthy, and she was so poor, she had no clothes to put on her son; so she used to fix him in the ash-hole, near the fire, and pile the warm ashes about him; and as he grew up, she sunk the pit deeper. At last, by hook or by crook, she got a goatskin, and fastened it round his waist, and he felt quite grand, and took a walk down the street. So says she to him next morning, " Tom, you thief, you never done any good yet, and you six foot high, and past nineteen;—take that rope, and bring me a *bresna* from the wood." " Never say't twice, mother," says Tom—" here goes."

When he had it gathered and tied, what should come up but a big giant, nine foot high, and made a lick of a club at him. Well become Tom, he jumped a-one side, and picked up a ram-pike; and the first crack he gave the big fellow, he made him kiss the clod. " If you have e'er a prayer," says Tom, " now's the time to say it, before I make *brishe* of you." " I know no prayers," says the giant; " but if you spare my life I'll give you that club; and as long as you keep from sin, you'll win every battle you ever fight with it."

Tom made no bones about letting him off; and as soon as he got the club in his hands, he sat down on the bresna, and gave it a tap with the kippeen, and says, " Bresna, I had a great trouble gathering you; the least you can do is to carry me home." And sure enough, the wind o' the word was all it wanted. It went off through the wood, groaning and cracking, till it came to the widow's door.

Well, when the sticks were all burned, Tom was sent off again to pick more; and this time he had to fight with a giant that had two heads on him. Tom had a little more trouble with him—that's all; and the prayers he said, was to give Tom a fife, that nobody could help dancing when he was playing it. Begonies, he made the big fagot dance home, with himself sitting on it. Well, if you were all the steps from this to Dublin, dickens a bit you'd ever arrive there. The next giant was a beautiful boy with three heads on him. He had neither prayer nor catechism no more nor the others; so he gave Tom a bottle of green ointment, that wouldn't let you be burned, nor scalded, nor wounded. " And now," says he, " there's none more of us. You may come and gather sticks here

26

till little *Lunacy Day* in Harvest, without giant or fairy-man to disturb you."

Well, now, Tom was prouder nor ten paycocks, and used to take a walk down the street in the heel of the evening; but some of the little boys had no more manners than if they were Dublin jackeens, and put out their tongues at Tom's club and Tom's goat-skin. He didn't like that at all, and it would be mean to give one of them a clout. last, what should come through the town but a kind of bellman, only it's a big bugle he had, and a huntsman's cap on his head. So this—he wasn't a bellman, and I don't know what to call him—bugleman, maybe, proclaimed that the King of Dublin's daughter was so melancholy that she didn't give a laugh for seven years, and that her father would grant her in marriage to whoever could make her laugh three times. " That's the very thing for me to try," says Tom; and so, without burning any more daylight, he kissed his mother, curled his club at the little boys, and off he set along the yalla highroad to the town of Dublin.

At last Tom came to one of the city gates, and the guards laughed and cursed at him instead of letting him in. Tom stood it all for a little time, but then one of them—out of fun, as he said—drove his bagnet half an inch or so into his side. Tom done nothing but take the fellow by the scruff o' the neck and the waistband of his corduroys, and fling him into the canal. Some run to pull the fellow out, and others to let manners into the vulgarian with their swords and daggers; but a tap from his club sent them headlong into the moat or down on the stones, and they were soon begging him to stay his hands.

So at last one of them was glad enough to show Tom the way to the palace-yard; and there was the king, and the queen, and the princess, in a gallery, looking at all sorts of wrestling, and sword-playing, and *rinka-fadhas*, and mumming, all to please the princess; but not a smile came over her handsome face.

Well, they all stopped when they saw the young giant, with his boy's face, and long black hair, and his short, curly beard—for his poor mother couldn't afford to buy razhurs—and his great strong arms, and bare legs, and no covering but the goatskin that reached from his waist to his knees. But an envious wizened fellow, with a red head, that wished to be married to the princess, and didn't like how she opened her eyes at Tom, came forward, and asked his business very snappishly. " My business," says Tom, " is to make the beautiful princess, God bless her, laugh three times." " Do you see all them merry fellows and skilful swordsmen," says the other, " that could eat you up with a grain of salt, and not a mother's soul of 'em ever got a laugh from her these seven years?" So the fellows gathered round Tom, and the bad man aggravated him till he told them he didn't care a pinch o' snuff for the whole bilin' of 'em; let them come on, six at a time, and try what they could do. The king that was too far off to hear what they were saying, asked what did the stranger want. "He wants," says the red-headed fellow, " to make hares of your best men." " Oh!" says the king, " if that's the way, let one of 'em

28

turn out and try his mettle." So one stood forward, with sword and pot-lid, and made a cut at Tom. He struck the fellow's elbow with the club, and up over their heads flew the sword, and down went the owner of it on the gravel from a thump he got on the helmet. Another took his place, and another, and another, and then half-dozen at once, and Tom sent sword, helmets, shields, and bodies rolling over and over, and themselves bawling out that they were killed, and disabled, and damaged, and rubbing their poor elbows and hips and limping away. Tom contrived not to kill any one; and the princess was so amused, that she let a great sweet laugh out of her that was heard all over the yard. " King of Dublin," says Tom, " I've quarter of your daughter." And the king didn't know whether he was glad or sorry, and all the blood in the princess's heart run into her cheeks.

So there was no more fighting that day, and Tom was invited to dine with the royal family. Next morning at breakfast Redhead told Tom of a wolf, the size of a yearling heifer, that used to be howling about the walls, and eating people and cattle; and said what a pleasure it would give the king to have it killed. " With all my heart," says Tom; " send a jackeen to show me where he lives, and we'll see how he behaves to a stranger." The princess was not well pleased, for Tom looked a different person with fine clothes and a nice green birredh over his long curly hair; and besides he'd got one laugh out of her. However, the king gave his consent; and in an hour and a half the horrible wolf was walking into the palace-yard, and Tom a step or two behind, with his club on his shoulder, just as a shepherd would be walking after a pet lamb.

The king and queen and princess were safe up in their gallery, but the officers and people of the court that were padrowling about the green bawn, when they saw the big baste coming in, gave themselves up, and began to make for doors and gates; and the wolf licked his chops, as if he was saying, " Wouldn't I enjoy a breakfast off a couple of yez!" The king shouted out, " O Gilla na Chreck an Gour, take away that terrible wolf, and you can have all my daughter." But Tom didn't mind him a bit. He pulled out his flute and began to play like vengeance; and dickens a man or boy in the yard but began shovelling away heel and toe, and the wolf himself was obliged to get on his hind legs and dance *Tatther Jack Walsh,* along with the rest. A good deal of people got inside, and shut the doors, the way the hairy fellow wouldn't pin them; but Tom kept playing, and the outsiders kept dancing and shouting and the wolf kept dancing and roaring with the pain his legs were giving him; and all the time he had his eyes on Redhead, who was shut out along with the rest. Wherever Redhead went, the wolf followed, and kept one eye on him and the other on Tom, to see if he would give him leave to eat him. But Tom shook his head, and never stopped the tune, and Redhead never stopped dancing and bawling, and the wolf dancing and roaring, one leg up and the other down, and he ready to drop out of his standing from fair tiresomeness.

When the princess seen that there was no fear of

30

any one being killed, she was so divarted by the stew that Redhead was in, that she gave another great laugh; and, well become Tom, out he cried, "King of Dublin, I have two halves of your daughter." "Oh, halves or alls," says the king, "put away that divel of a wolf, and we'll see about it." So Gilla put his flute in his pocket, and says he to the baste that was sittin' on his *currabingo* ready to faint, "Walk off to your mountain, my fine fellow, and live like a respectable baste; and if I ever find you come within seven miles of any town, I'll—." He said no more, but spit in his fist, and gave a flourish of his club. It was all the poor divel wanted: he put his tail between his legs, and took to his pumps without looking at man or mortal, and neither sun, moon, nor stars ever saw him in sight of Dublin again.

At dinner every one laughed but the foxy fellow; and sure enough he was laying out how he'd settle poor Tom next day. "Well, to be sure!" says he, "King of Dublin, you are in luck. There's the Danes moidhering us to no end. D—— run to Lusk wid 'em! and if any one can save us from 'em, it is this gentleman with the goatskin. There is a flail hangin' on the collar-beam in hell, and neither Dane nor devil can stand before it." "So," says Tom to the king, "will you let me have the other half of the princess if I bring you the flail?" "No, no," says the princess; "I'd rather never be your wife than see you in that danger." But Redhead whispered and nudged Tom about how shabby it would look to renegue the adventure. So he asked which way he was to go, and Redhead directed him through a street where a great many bad women lived, and a great many shebeen houses were open, and away he set.

Well, he travelled and travelled, till he came in sight of the walls of hell; and, bedad, before he knocked at the gates, he rubbed himself over with the greenish ointment. When he knocked, a hundred little imps popped their heads out through the bars, and asked him what he wanted. " Open the gate," says Tom: " I want to speak to the big divel of all."

It wasn't long till the gate was thrown open, and the Ould Boy received Tom with bows and scrapes, and asked his business. " My business isn't much," says Tom. " I only came for the loan of that flail that I see hanging on the collar-beam, for the King of Dublin to give a thrashing to the Danes." " Well," says the other, " the Danes are much better customers to me; but since you walked so far I won't refuse. Hand that flail," says he to a young imp; and he winked the far-off eye at the same time. So, while some were barring the gates, the young divel climbed up, and took down the flail that had the handstaff and *booltheen* both made out of red-hot iron. The little vagabond was grinning to think how it would burn the hands off o' Tom, but the dickens a burn it made on him, no more if it was a good oak sapling. " Thankee," says Tom. " Now would you open the gate for a body, and I'll give you no more trouble." " Oh, tramp!" says Ould Nick; " is that the way? It is easier getting inside them gates than getting out again. Take that tool from him, and give him a dose of the oil of stirrup." So one fellow put out his claws to seize on the flail, but Tom gave him

32

such a welt of it and made him roar like a devil as he was. Well, they all rushed at Tom but he gave them, little and big, such a thrashing as they didn't forget for a while. At last says the old thief rubbing his elbow, " Let the fool out; and woe to whoever lets him in again, great or small."

So out marched Tom, without minding the shouting and cursing they kept up at him from the tops of the walls; and when he got home to the big bawn of the palace, there was never such running and racing as to see himself and the flail. When he had his story told, he laid down the flail on the stone steps, and bid no one for their lives to touch it. If the king, and queen, and princess made much of him before, they made ten times more of him now; but Redhead, the mean scruff-bound, stole over, and thought to catch hold of the flail to make an end of him. His fingers hardly touched it, when he let a roar out of him as if heaven and earth were coming together, and kept flinging his arms about and dancing, that it was pitiful to look at him. Tom ran at him as soon as he could rise, caught his hands in his own two, and rubbed them this way and that, and the burning pain left them before you could reckon one. Well, the poor fellow, between the pain that was only just gone, and the comfort he was in, had the comicalest face that ever you see. It was such a mixtherum-gatherum of laughing and crying and everybody burst out a-laughing—and the princess could not stop no more than the rest; and then says Gilla, or Tom, " Now, ma'am, if there were fifty halves of you, I hope you'll give me them all." Well, the princess had no mock modesty about her. She looked at her father, and by my word, she came over to Gilla, and put her two delicate hands into his rough ones, and I wish it was myself was in his shoes that day!

Tom would not bring the flail into the palace. You may be sure no other body went near it; and when the early risers next morning were passing, they found two long clefts in the stone, where it was after burning itself an opening downwards, nobody could tell how far. But a messenger came in at noon and said that the Danes were so frightened when they heard of the flail coming into Dublin, that they got into their ships, and sailed away.

Well, I suppose, before they were married, Gilla got some man, like Pat Mara of Tomenine, to larn him the " Principles of politeness, fluxions, gunnery and fortification, decimal fractions, practice, and the rule of three direct," the way he'd be able to keep up a conversation with the royal family. Whether he ever lost his time, larning them sciences, I'm not sure, but it's as sure as fate that his mother never more saw any want till the end of her days.

Jack the Master and Jack the Servant

There was once a poor couple, and they had three sons, and the youngest's name was Jack. One harvest day, the eldest fellow threw down his hook, and says he, " What's the use to be slaving this way? I'll go seek my fortune." And the second son said the very same; and says Jack, " I'll go seek my fortune along with you, but let us first leave the harvest stacked for the old couple." Well, he over-persuaded them, and bedad, as soon as it was safe, they kissed their father and mother, and off they set, every one with three pounds in his pocket, promising to be home in a year and a day. The first night they found no better lodging than a fine dry dyke of a ditch, out-side of a churchyard. Before they went to sleep, the youngest got inside to read the tombstone and what should he stumble over but a coffin and the sod was just taken off where the grave was to be. " Some poor body," says he, " that was without friends to put him in consecrated ground : he mustn't be left this way." So he threw off his coat, and had a couple of feet cleared out, when a terrible giant walked up. " What are you at?" says he. " The corpse owed me a guinea, and he shan't be buried till it is paid." " Well, here is your guinea," says Jack, " and leave the church-yard, it's nothing the better for your company." Well, he got down a couple of feet more, when another uglier giant again, with two heads on him, came and stopped Jack with the same story, and got his guinea; and when the grave was six feet down, the third giant looks on him and he had three heads. So Jack was obliged to part with his three guineas before he could put the sod over the poor man. Then he went and lay down by his brothers, and slept till the sun began to shine on their faces next morning.

Well, they soon came to a cross-roads, and there

every one took his own way. Jack told them how all his money was gone, but not a farthing did they offer him. After some time, Jack found himself hungry, and so he sat down by the roadside, and pulled out a piece of cake and a lump of bacon. Just as he had the first bit in his mouth, up comes a poor man, and asks something of him, for God's sake. " I have neither brass, gold, nor silver about me," says Jack; " and here's all the provisions I'm master of. Sit down and have a share." Well, the poor man didn't require much pressing, and when the meal was over, says he, " Sir, where are you bound for?" " Faith, I don't know," says Jack; " I'm going to seek my fortune." " I'll go with you for your servant," says the other. " Servant indeed! bad I want a servant—I, that's looking out for a place myself." " No matter. You gave Christian burial to my poor brother yesterday evening. He appeared to me in a dream, and told me where I'd find you, and that I was to be your servant for a year. So you'll be Jack the master, and I Jack the servant." " Well, let it be so."

After sunset, they came to a castle in a wood, and " Here," says the servant, " lives the giant with one head, that wouldn't let my poor brother be buried." He took hold of a club that hung by the door, and gave two or three thravallys on it. " What do you want?" says the giant, looking out through a grating. " Oh, sir, honey!" says Jack, " we want to save you. The king is sending 100,000 men to take your life for all the wickedness you ever done to poor travellers, and that. So because you let my brother be buried, I came to help you." " Oh, murdher, murdher, what'll I do at all, at all?" says he. "Have you e'er a hiding-place?" says Jack. "I have a cave seven miles long, and it opens into the bawn." "That'll do. Leave a good supper for the men, and then don't stir out of your pew till I call you." So they went in, and the giant left a good supper for the army, and went down, and they shut the trap-door down on him.

Well, they ate and they drank, and then Jack got all the horses and cows, and drove them over an hether the trapdoor, and such fighting and shouting, whinnying and lowing as they had and such a noise as they made! Then Jack opened the door and called out, "Are you there, sir?" "I am," says he, from a mile or two inside. "Wor you frightened, sir?" "You may say frightened. Are they gone away?" "Dickens a go they'll go till you give them your sword of sharpness." "Cock them up with the sword of sharpness. I won't give them a smite of it." "Well, I think you're right. Look out. They'll be down with you in the twinkling of a harrow pin. Go to the end of the cave, and they won't have your head for an hour to come." "Well, that's no great odds; you'll find it in the closet inside the parlour. D —— do 'em good with it." "Very well," says Jack; "when they're all cleared off, I'll drop a big stone on the trap-door." So the two Jacks slept very comfortable in the giant's bed—it was big enough for the two of them; and next morning, after breakfast, they dropped the big stone on the trap-door, and away they went.

That night they slept at the castle of the two-headed giant, and got his cloak of darkness in the same way; and the next night they slept at the castle of the three-headed giant, and got his shoes of swiftness; and the next night they were near the king's palace. "Now," says Jack the servant, "this king has a daughter, and she was so proud that eleven princes killed themselves for her, because she would not marry any of them. At last the King of Morocco thought to persuade her, and the dickens a bit of him she'd have no more nor the others. So he fell on his sword, and died; and the old boy got leave to give him a kind of life again, to punish the proud lady, and he lives in a palace one side of the river, and the king's palace is on the other, and he has got power over the princess and her father; and when they have the heads of twelve courtiers over the gates, the King of Morocco will have the princess to himself and maybe the evil spirit will have them both. Every young man that offers himself has to do three things, and if he fails in all, up goes his head. There you see them—eleven, all black and white, with the sun and rain. You must try your hand. God is stronger than the devil."

So they came to the gate. "What do you want?" says the guard. "I want to marry the princess." "Do you see them heads? Yours will be along with them before you're a week older." "That's my own look out," says Jack. "Well, go on. God help all foolish people!" The king was on his throne in the big hall, and the princess sitting on a golden chair by his side. "Death or my daughter, I suppose," says the king to Jack the master. "Just so, my liege," says Jack. "Very well," says the king. " I don't know whether I'm glad or sorry," says he. " If you don't succeed in three things, my daughter must marry the King of Morocco. If you do succeed, I suppose we'll be eased from the dog's life we are leading. I'll leave my daughter's scissors in your bedroom to-night, and you'll find no one going in till morning. If you have the scissors still at sunrise, your head will be safe for that day. Next day you must run a race against the King of Morocco, and if you win, your head will be safe that day too. Next day you must bring me the King of Morocco's head, or your own head, then all this bother will be over one way or the other."

Well, they gave the two a good supper, and one time the princess would look sweet at Jack, and another sour; for you know she was under enchantment. Sometimes she'd wish him killed, sometimes she'd like him to be saved.

When they went into their bedroom, the king came in with them, and laid the scissors on the table. " Mind that," says he, " and I'm sure I don't know whether I wish to find it there to-morrow or not." Well, poor Jack was a little frightened, but his man encouraged him. " Go to bed," says he; " I'll put on the cloak of darkness, and watch, and I hope you'll find the scissors there at sunrise." Well, bedad he couldn't go to sleep; he kept his eyes on the scissors till the dead hour, and the moment it struck twelve no scissors could he see : it vanished as clean as a whistle. He looked here, there, and everywhere—no scissors. " Well," says he, " there's hope still. Are you there, Jack?" but no answer came. " I can do no more," says he. " I'll go to bed." And to bed he went, and slept.

Just as the clock was striking, Jack in the cloak saw the wall opening, and the princess walking in, going over to the table, taking up the scissors, and walking out again. He followed her into the garden, and there he saw herself and her twelve maids going down to the boat that was lying by the bank. " I'm in," says the princess. " I'm in," says one maid; and " I'm in," says another; and so on till all were in; " and I'm in," says Jack. " Who's that?" says the last maid. " Go look," says Jack. Well, they were all a bit frightened. When they got over, they walked up to the King of Morocco's palace, and there the King of Morocco was to receive them, and give them the best of eating and drinking, and make his musicians play the finest music for them.

When they were coming away, says the princess, " Here's the scissors; mind it or not as you like." " Oh, won't I mind it!" says he. " Here you go," says he again, opening a chest, and dropping it into it, and locking it up with three locks. But before he shut down the lid, Jack in the cloak picked up the scissors, and put it safe into his pocket. Well, when they came to the boat, the same things were said, and the maids were frightened again.

When Jack the master awoke in the morning, the first thing he saw was the scissors on the table, and the next thing he saw was his man lying asleep in the other bed, the next was the cloak of darkness hanging on the bed's foot. Well, he got up, and he danced, and he sung, and he hugged Jack; and when the king came in with a troubled face, there was the scissors safe and sound. " Well, Jack," says he, "you're safe for one day more." And the king and princess were more *meentrach* to Jack to-day than they were yesterday, but the next day the race was to be run.

At last the hour of noon came, and there was the King of Morocco with his hair and his eyes as black as a crow, and his face as yellow as a kite's claw. Jack was there too, and on his feet were the shoes of swiftness. When the bugle blew, they were off, and Jack went seven times round the course while the king went one: it was like the fish in the water, the arrow from a bow, the stone from a sling, or a star shooting in the night. When the race was won, and the people were shouting, the black king looked at Jack like the very devil himself, and says he: "Don't holloa till you're out of the wood —to-morrow your head or mine." "Heaven is stronger than hell," says Jack.

And now the princess began to wish in earnest that Jack would win, for two parts of the charm were broke. So one of her maids told Jack the servant that she should pay her visit to the Black Fellow at midnight like every other night past. Jack in the cloak was in the garden when the hour came, and they all said the same words, and rowed over, and went up to the palace like they done before.

The King of Morocco was in a great fear and anger, and scolded the princess, but she didn't seem to mind it, and when they were leaving she said, "You know to-morrow is to have your head or Jack's head off. I suppose you will stay up all night!" He was standing on the grass when they were getting into the boat, and just as the last maid had the foot on the edge of it, Jack the servant swept off his head with the sword of sharpness just as if it was the head of a thistle, and put it under his cloak. The body fell on the grass and made no noise. Well, the same moment the princess felt any liking she had for him all gone like last year's snow, and she began to sob and cry for fear of anything happening to Jack. But the maids were not very good at all, and so, from the moment they got out of the boat, Jack kept knocking the head against their faces and their legs, and made them roar and bawl till they were inside the palace.

The first thing Jack the master saw when he woke in the morning, was the black head on the table, and didn't he jump up in a hurry. When the sun was rising, every one in the palace, great and small, were in the bawn before Jack's window, and the king was at the door. " Jack," says he, " if you haven't the King of Morocco's head on a gad, your own will be on a spear, my poor fellow." But just at the moment he. heard a great shout from the bawn, and Jack the servant was after opening the window, holding out the King of Morocco's head by the long black hair.

So the princess, and the king, and all were in joy, and maybe they didn't keep the wedding long a-waiting. A year and a day after Jack left home, himself and his wife were in their coach at the cross-roads, and there were the two brothers, sleeping in the ditch with their reaping-hooks by their sides. They wouldn't believe Jack at first that he was their brother, and then they were ready to eat their nails for not sharing with him that day twelve-month. They found their father and mother alive, and you may be sure they left them comfortable. So you see what a good thing in the end it is to be charitable to the poor, dead or alive.

I'll Be Wiser Next Time

Jack was twenty years old before he had done any good for his family. So at last his mother said it was high time for him to begin to be of some use. So the next market day she sent him to Bunclody to buy a billhook to cut the furze. When he was coming back he kept cutting *gaaches* with it round his head, till at last it flew out of his hands, and killed a lamb that a neighbour was bringing home. Well, if he did, so sure was his mother obliged to pay for it, and Jack was in disgrace. "Musha, you fool," says she, "couldn't you lay the billhook in a car, or stick it into a bundle of hay or straw that any of the neighbours would be bringing home?" "Well, mother," says he, "it can't be helped now; I'll be wiser the next time."

"Now, Jack," says she, the next Sunday, "you behaved like a fool the last time; have some wit about you now and don't get us into a hobble. Here is a fi'penny bit, and buy me a good pair of knitting needles, and fetch them home safe." "Never fear, mother." When Jack was outside the town, coming back, he overtook a neighbour sitting on the side-lace of his car, and there was a big bundle of hay in the bottom of it. "Just the safe thing," says Jack, sticking the needles into it. When

43

he came home he looked quite proud of his management. " Well, Jack," says his mother, " where's the needles?" " Oh, faith; they're safe enough. Send any one down to Jem Doyle's, and he'll find them in the bundle of hay that's in the car." " Musha, purshuin to you, Jack! Why couldn't you stick them into the band o' your hat? What searching there will be for them in the hay!" " Sure you said I ought to put any things I was bringing home in a car, or stick 'em in hay or straw. Anyhow, I'll be wiser next time."

Next week Jack was sent to a neighbour's house about a mile away, for some of her nice fresh butter. The day was hot, and Jack remembering his mother's words, stuck the cabbage leaf that held the butter between his hat and the band. He was luckier this turn than the other turns, for he brought his errand safe in his hair and down along his clothes. There's no pleasing some people, however, and his mother was so vexed that she was ready to beat him.

There was so little respect for Jack's gumption in the whole village after this, that he wasn't let go to market for a fortnight. Then his mother trusted him with a pair of young fowl. " Now don't be too eager to snap at the first offer you'll get; wait for the second any way, and above all things keep your wits about you." Jack got to the market safe. " How do you sell them fowl, honest boy?" " My mother bid me a three shillings for 'em, but sure herself said I wouldn't get it." " She never said a truer word. Will you have eighteen pence?" " In troth an' I won't; she ordhered me to wait for a second offer." " And very wisely she acted; here

is a shilling." " Well, now, I think it would be
wiser to take the eighteen pence, but it is better
for me at any rate to go by her bidding, and then
she can't blame me."

Jack was in disgrace for three weeks after making that bargain; and some of the neighbours went
so far as to say that Jack's mother didn't show
much more wit than Jack himself.

She had to send him, however, next market day
to sell a young sheep, and says she to him, " Jack,
I'll have your life if you don't get the highest penny
in the market for that baste." " Oh, won't I?" says
Jack. Well, when he was standing in the market,
up comes a jobber, asks him what he'd take for the
sheep. " My mother won't be satisfied," says Jack,
" if I don't bring her home the highest penny in
the market." " Will a guinea note do you?" says
the other. ". Is it the highest penny in the market?"
says Jack. " No, but here's the highest penny in
the market," says a sleeveen that was listenin',
getting up on a high ladder that was restin' again'
the market house : " here's the highest penny, and
the sheep is mine."

Well, if the poor mother wasn't heart-scalded
this time it's no matter. She said she'd never lose
more than a shilling a turn by him again while she
lived; but she had to send him for some groceries
next Saturday for all that, for it was Christmas
Eve. " Now, Jack," says she, " I want some cinnamon, mace and cloves, and half a pound of raisins;
will you be able to think o' 'em?" " Able, indeed;
I'll be repatin' 'em every inch o' the way, and that
won't let me forget them." So he never stopped as
he ran along, saying " cinnamon, mace and cloves,

45

and half a pound of raisins "; and this time he'd come home in glory, only he struck his foot again' a stone, and fell down, and hurt himself.

At last he got up, and as he went limping on he strove to remember his errand, but it was changed in his mind to " pitch, and tar and turpentine, and half a yard of sacking "—" pitch, and tar, and turpentine, and half a yard of sacking." These did not help the Christmas dinner much, and his mother was so tired of minding him that she sent him along with a clever black man up to the County Carlow, to get a wife to take care of him.

Well, the black man never let him open the mouth all the time the coorting was goin' on; and at last the whole party—his friends and her friends —were gathered into the priest's parlour. The black man stayed close to him for 'fraid he'd do a bull; and when Jack was married half-a-year, if he thought his life was bad enough before, he thought it ten times worse now; and told his mother if she'd send his wife back to her father, he'd never make a mistake again going to fair or market. But the wife cock-crowed over the mother as well as over Jack; and if they didn't live happy, THAT WE MAY.

The Three Crowns

There was once a king, some place or other, and he had three daughters. The two eldest were very proud and uncharitable, but the youngest was as good as they were bad. Well, three princes came to court them, and two of them were the moral of the eldest ladies, and one was just as lovable as the youngest. They were all walking down to a lake one day that lay at the bottom of the lawn, just like the one at Castleboro', and they met a poor beggar. The king wouldn't give him anything, and the eldest princes wouldn't give him anything, nor their sweethearts; but the youngest daughter and her true love did give something, and the kind words along with it, and that was better nor all.

When they got to the edge of the lake, what did they find but the beautifullest boat you ever saw in your life; and, says the eldest, " I'll take a sail in this fine boat "; and, says the second eldest, " I'll take a sail in this fine boat "; and, says the youngest, " I won't take a sail in that fine boat, for I am afraid it's an enchanted one." But the others over-persuaded her to go in, and her father was just going after her, when up sprung on the deck a little man only seven inches high, and he ordered him to stand back. Well, all the men put their hands to their soords; and if the same soords were only *thraneens* they weren't able to draw them, for all the strength had left their arms. Seven Inches loosened the silver chain that fastened the boat, and pushed away; and after grinning at the four men, says he to them, " Bid your daughters and your brides farewell for awhile. That wouldn't have happened you three, only for your want of charity. You," says he to the youngest, " needn't fear, you'll recover your princess all in good time, and you and she will be as happy as the day is long. Bad people, if they were rolling stark naked in gold,

47

would not be rich. *Banacht lath*." Away they sailed, and the ladies stretched out their hands but 'weren't able to say a word.

Well, they weren't crossing the lake while a cat 'ud be lickin' her ear, and the poor men couldn't stir hand or foot to follow them. They saw Seven Inches handing the three princesses out o' the boat, and letting them down by a nice basket and windlass into a draw-well that was convenient, but nor king nor princes ever saw an opening before in the same place. When the last lady was out of sight, the men found the strength in their arms and legs again. Round the lake they ran, and never drew rein till they came to the well and windlass; and there was the silk rope rolled on the axle, and the nice white basket hanging to it. " Let me down," says the youngest prince; " I'll die or recover them again." " No," says the second's sweetheart, " I'm entitled to my turn before you." And says the other, " I must get first turn, in right of my bride." So they gave way to him, and he got to the basket, and down they let him. First they lost sight of him, and then, after winding off a hundred perches of silk rope, it slackened, and they stopped turning. They waited two hours, and then they went to dinner, because there was no chuck made at the rope.

Guards were set till next morning, and then down went the second prince, and sure enough, the youngest of all got himself let down on the third day. He went down perches and perches, while it was as dark about him as if he was in a big pot with the cover on. At last he saw a glimmer far down, and in a short time he felt the ground. Out he came from the big lime-kiln, and lo and behold! there was a wood, and a green field, and a castle in a lawn, and a bright sky over all. "It's in Tir-na-n-Oge I am," says he. "Let's see what sort of people are in the castle." On he walked, across fields and lawn, and no one was there to keep him out or let him into the castle. But the big hall door was wide open. He went from one fine room to another that was finer, and at last he reached the handsomest of all, with a table in the middle : and such a dinner was laid upon it! The prince felt hungry enough, but he was too mannerly to go eat without being invited. So he sat by the fire, and he did not wait long till he heard steps, and in came Seven Inches and the youngest sister by the hand. Well, prince and princess flew into one another's arms, and says the little man, says he, "Why aren't you eating?" "I think, sir," says he, "it was only good manners to wait to be asked." "The other princes didn't think so," says he. "Each o' them fell to without leave or licence, and only gave me the rough side o' their tongue when I told them they were making more free than welcome. Well, I don't think they feel much hunger now. There they are, good marble instead of flesh and blood," says he, pointing to two statues, one in one corner, and the other in the other corner of the room. The prince was frightened, but he was afraid to say anything, and Seven Inches made him sit down to dinner between himself and his bride; and he'd be as happy as the day long, only for the sight of the stone men in the corner. Well, that day went by, and when the next came, says Seven Inches to him : "Now, you'll have to set out that way," pointing to the sun;

" and you'll find the second princess in a giant's castle this evening, when you'll be tired and hungry, and the eldest princess to-morrow evening; and you may as well bring them here with you. I suppose, if they ever get home, they'll look on poor people as if they were flesh and blood like themselves."

Away went the prince, and bedad, it's tired and hungry he was when he reached the first castle, at sunset. Oh, wasn't the second princess glad to see him! and if she didn't give him a good supper, it's a wonder. But she heard the giant at the gate, and she hid the prince in a closet. Well, when he came in, he snuffed, an' says he, " Be the life, I smell fresh mate." " Oh," says the princess, " it's only the calf I got killed to-day." " Ay, ay," says he, " is supper ready?" " It is," says she; and before he ruz from the table he hid three-quarters of the calf, and a cag of wine. " I think," says he, when all was done, " I smell fresh mate still." " It's sleepy you are," says she, " go to bed." " When will you marry me?" says the giant. " You're puttin' me off too long." " St. Tibb's Eve," says she. " I wish I knew how far off that is," says he; and he fell asleep, with his head in the dish. Next day, he went out after breakfast, and she sent the prince to the castle where the eldest sister was. The same thing happened there; but when the giant was snoring, the princess wakened up the prince, and they saddled two steeds in the stables, and *magh go bragh* with them. But the horses' heels struck the stones outside the gate, and up got the giant, and after them he made. He roared and shouted, and the more he shouted the faster ran the horses; and just as the day was breaking, he was only twenty perches behind. But the prince didn't leave the castle of Seven Inches without being provided with something good. He reined in his steed, and flung a short, sharp knife over his shoulder, and up sprung a thick wood between the giant and themselves. They caught the wind that blew before them, and the wind that blew behind them did not catch them. At last they were near the castle where the other sister lived; and there she was, waiting for them under a high hedge, and a fine steed under her.

But the giant was now in sight, roaring like a hundred lions, and the other was out in a moment, and the chase kept on. For every two springs the horses gave, the giants gave three, and at last they were only seventy perches off. Then the prince stopped again, and flung the second *skian* behind him. Down went all the flat field, till there was a quarry between them a quarter of a mile deep, and the bottom filled with black water; and before the giants could get round it, the prince and princesses were inside the domain of the great magician, where the high thorny hedge opened itself to every one that he chose to let in.

Well, to be sure, there was joy enough between the three sisters, till the two eldest saw their lovers turned into stone. But while they were shedding tears for them, Seven Inches came in, and touched them with his rod. So they were flesh, and blood, and life once more, and there was great hugging and kissing, and all sat down to a nice breakfast and Seven Inches sat at the head of the table.

When breakfast was over, he took them into another room where there was nothing but heaps of gold, and silver, and diamonds, and silks, and satins; and on a table there was lying three sets of crowns: a gold crown was in a silver crown, and that was lying in a copper crown. He took up one set of crowns and gave it to the eldest princess; and another set, and gave it to the second princess; and another and gave it to the youngest of all; and says he, " Now you may all go to the bottom of the pit, and you have nothing to do but stir the basket, and the people that are watching above will draw you up. But remember, ladies, you are to keep your crowns safe, and be married in them, all the same day. If you be married separately, or if you be married without your crowns, a curse will follow—mind what I say."

So they took leave of him with great respect, and walked arm-in-arm to the bottom of the draw-well. There was a sky and a sun over them, and a great high wall, covered with ivy, rose before them, and was so high they couldn't see to the top of it; and there was an arch in this wall, and the bottom of the draw-well was inside the arch. The youngest pair went last; and says the princess to the prince, " I'm so sure the two princes don't mean any good to you. Keep these crowns under your cloak, and if you are obliged to stay last, don't get into the basket, but put a big stone, or any heavy thing inside and see what will happen."

So, when they were inside the dark cave, they put the eldest princess first, and stirred the basket, and up she went, but first she gave a little scream.

52

Then the basket was let down again, and up went the second princess, and then went up the youngest; but first she put her arms round her prince's neck, and kissed him, and cried a little. At last it came to the turn of the youngest prince, and well became him;—instead of going into the basket, he put in a big stone. He drew on one side and listened, and after the basket was drawn up about twenty perch, down came itself and the stone like thunder, and the stone was *brishe* of on the flags.

Well, my poor prince had nothing for it but to walk back to the castle; and through it and round it he walked, and the finest of eating and drinking he got, and a bed of bog-down to sleep on, and fine walks he took through gardens and lawns, but not a sight could he get, high or low, of Seven Inches. Well, I don't think any of us would be tired of this fine way of living for ever. Maybe we would. Anyhow the prince got tired of it before a week, he was so lonesome for his true love; and at the end of a month he didn't know what to do with himself. So one morning he went into the treasure-room, and took notice of a beautiful snuff-box on the table that he didn't remember seeing there before. He took it in his hands and opened it, and out Seven Inches walked on the table. " I think, prince," says he, " you're getting a little tired of my castle?" "Ah!" says the other, " if I had my princess here, and could see you now and then, I'd never see a dismal day." " Well, you're long enough here now, and you're wanting there above. Keep your bride's crowns safe, and whenever you want my help, open this snuff-box.

Now take a walk down the garden, and come back when you're tired."

Well, the prince was going down a gravel walk with a quickset hedge on each side, and his eyes on the ground, and he thinking on one thing and another. At last he lifted his eyes, and there he was outside of a smith's bawn-gate that he often passed before, about a mile away from the palace of his betrothed princess. The clothes he had on him were as ragged as you please, but he had his crowns safe under his cloak.

So the smith came out, and says he, "It's a shame for a strong, big fellow like you to be on the *sthra,* and so much work to be done. Are you any good with hammer and tongs? Come in and bear a hand, and I'll give you diet and lodging, and a few thirteens when you earn them." "Never say't twice," says the prince; "I want nothing but to be employed." So he took the sledge, and pounded away at the red-hot bar that the smith was turning on the anvil to make into a set of horse-shoes.

Well, they weren't long powdhering away, when a *sthronshuch* of a tailor came in; and when the smith asked him what news he had, he got the handle of the bellows and began to blow, to let out all he had for the last two days. There was so many questions and answers at first, that if I told them all, it would be bedtime afore I'd be done. So here is the substance of the discourse; and before he got far into it, the forge was half-filled with women knitting stockings, and men smoking.

"Yous all heard how the two princesses were

54

unwilling to be married till the ycungest would be ready with her crowns and her sweetheart. But after the windlass loosened accidentally when they were pulling up her bridegroom that was to be, there was no more sign of a well, a rope, or a windlass, than there is on the palm of your hand. So the buckeens that wor coortin' the eldest ladies, wouldn't give peace or ease to their lovers nor the king, till they got consent to the marriage, and it was to take place this morning. Myself went down out o' curiosity; and to be sure I was delighted with the grand dresses of the two brides, and the three crowns on their heads—gold, silver, and copper, one inside the other. The youngest was standing by mournful enough in white, and all was ready. The two bridegrooms came in as proud and grand as you please, and up they were walking to the altar rails, when, my dear, the boards opened two yards under their feet, and down they went among the dead men and the coffins in the vaults. Oh, such screeching as the ladies gave! and such running and racing and peeping down there was; but the clerk soon opened the door of the vault, and up came the two heroes, and their fine clothes covered an inch thick with cobwebs and mould."

So the king said they should put off the marriage. " For," says he, " I see there is no use in thinking of it till my youngest is married along with the others. I'll give my youngest daughter for a wife to whoever brings three crowns to me like the others; and if he doesn't care to be married, some other one will, and I'll make his fortune." " I wish," says the smith, " I could do it: but I was looking at the crowns after the

55

princesses got home, and I don't think there's a black or a white smith on the face o' the earth could imitate them." "Faint heart never won fair lady," says the prince. "Go to the palace and ask for a quarter of a pound of gold, a quarter of a pound of silver, and a quarter of a pound of copper. Get one crown for a pattern; and my head for a pledge, I'll give you out the very things that are wanted in the morning." "Ubba-bow!" says the smith, "are you in earnest?" "Faith, I am so," says he. "Go! worse than lose you can't."

To make a long story short, the smith got the quarter of a pound of gold, and the quarter of a pound of silver, and the quarter of a pound of copper, and gave them and the pattern crown to the prince. He shut the forge door at nightfall, and the neighbours all gathered in the bawn, and they heard him hammering, hammering, hammering, from that to daybreak; and every now and then he'd pitch out through the window bits of gold, silver and copper; and the idlers scrambled for them, and cursed one another, and prayed for the good luck of the workman.

Well, just as the sun was thinking to rise, he opened the door and brought out the three crowns he got from his true love, and such shouting and huzzaing as there was! The smith asked him to go along with him to the palace, but he refused; so off set the smith, and the whole townland with him; and wasn't the king rejoiced when he saw the crowns! "Well," says he to the smith, "you're a married man; what's to be done?" "Faith, your majesty, I didn't make them crowns at all; it was

56

a big *shuler* of a fellow that took employment with me yesterday." " Well, daughter, will you marry the fellow that made these crowns?" " Let me see them first, father." So when she examined them, she knew them right well, and guessed it was her true-love that sent them. " I will marry the man that these crowns came from," says she.

" Well," says the king to the eldest of the two princes, " go up to the smith's forge, take my best coach, and bring home the bridegroom." He was very unwilling to do this, he was so proud, but he did not wish to refuse. When he came to the forge, he saw the prince standing at the door, and beckoned him over to the coach. " Are you the fellow," says he, " that made them crowns?" " Yes," says the other. " Then," says he, " maybe you'd give yourself a brushing, and get into that coach; the king wants to see you. I pity the princess." The young prince got into the carriage, and while they were on the way, he opened the snuff-box, and out walked Seven Inches, and stood on his thigh. " Well," says he, " what trouble is on you now?" " Master," says the other. " Please let me be back in my forge, and let this carriage be filled with paving stones." No sooner said than done. The prince was sitting in his forge, and the horses wondered what was after happening to the carriage.

When they came into the palace yard, the king himself opened the carriage door, to pay respect to his new son-in-law. As soon as he turned the handle, a shower of small stones fell on his powdered wig and his silk coat, and down he fell under them. There was great fright and some titter-

57

ing, and the king, after he wiped the blood from his forehead, looked very cross at the eldest prince. "My liege," says he, "I am very sorry for this accident, but I'm not to blame. I saw the young smith get into the carriage and we never stopped a minute since." "It's uncivil you were to him. Go," says he, to the other prince, "and bring the young smith here, and be polite." "Never fear," says he. But there's some people that couldn't be good-natured if they were to be made heirs of Damer's estate. Not a bit civiller was the new messenger than the old, and when the king opened the carriage door a second time, it's a shower of mud that came down on him; and if he didn't fume, and splutter, and shake himself, it's no matter. "There's no use," says he, "going on this way, the fox never got a better messenger than himself."

So he changed his clothes and washed himself, and out he set to the smith's forge. Maybe he wasn't polite to the young prince, and asked him to sit along with himself. But the young prince begged to be allowed to sit in the other carriage, and when they were half-way, he opened his snuff-box. "Master," says he, "I wish to be dressed now according to my rank." "You shall be that," says Seven Inches. "And now I'll bid you farewell. Continue as good and kind as you always were; and love your wife, and that's all the advice I'll give you." So Seven Inches vanished; and when the carriage door was opened in the yard—not by the king though, for a burnt child dreads the fire—out walks the prince as fine as pins and hands could make him, and the first thing he did was to run over to his bride, and embrace her very heartily.

Every one had great joy but the two other princes. There was not much delay about the marriages that were all celebrated on one day. Soon after, the two elder couples went to their own courts, but the youngest pair stayed with the old king, and they were as happy as the happiest married couple you ever heard of in a story.

The Corpse Watchers

There was once a poor woman that had three daughters, and one day the eldest said, " Mother, bake my cake and kill my cock, till I go seek my fortune." So she did, and when all was ready, says her mother to her, " Which will you have—half of these with my blessing, or the whole with my curse?" " Curse or no curse," says she, " the whole is little enough." So away she set, and if the mother didn't give her her curse, she didn't give her her blessing.

She walked and she walked till she was tired and hungry, and then she sat down to take her dinner. While she was eating, a poor woman came up, and asked for a bit. " The dickens a bit you'll get from me," says she; " it's all too little for myself," and the poor woman walked away very sorrowful. At nightfall she got lodging at a farmer's, and the woman of the house told her that she'd give her a spadeful of gold and a shovelful of silver if she'd only sit up and watch her son's corpse that was waking in the next room. She said she'd do that; and so when the family were in their bed, she sat by the fire, and cast an eye from time to time on the corpse that was lying under the table.

All at once the dead man got up in his shroud, and stood before her, and said, " All alone, fair maid!" She gave him no answer, and when he said it a third time, he struck her with a switch, and she became a grey flag.

About a week after, the second daughter went to seek her fortune, and she didn't care for her mother's blessing no more nor her sister, and the very thing happened to her. She was left a grey flag by the side of the other.

At last the youngest went off in search of the other two, and she took her mother's blessing with her. She shared her dinner with the poor woman on the road who told her that she would watch over her.

Well, she got lodging in the same place as the others, and agreed to mind the corpse. She sat up by the fire, with the dog and cat, and amused herself with some apples and nuts the mistress gave her. She thought it a pity that the man under the table was a corpse, he was so handsome.

But at last he got up, and says he, " All alone, fair maid!" and she wasn't long about an answer : —

" All alone I am not,
I've little dog Douse and Pussy, my cat;
I've apples to roast, and nuts to crack,
and all alone I'm not."

" Ho, ho!" says he, " you're a girl of courage,

though you wouldn't have enough to follow me. I am now going to cross the quaking bog, and go through the burning forest. I must then enter the grave of terror, and climb the hill of glass, and drop from the top of it into the Dead Sea." " I'll follow you," says she, " for I promised to mind you." He thought to prevent her, but she was as stiff as he was stout.

Out he sprang through the window, and she followed him till they came to the " Green Hills," and then says he :—

. " Open, open, Green Hills, and let the Light of the Green Hills through;"

" Aye," says the girl, " and let the fair maid, too."

They opened, and the man and woman passed through, and there they were, on the edge of a bog.

He trod lightly over the shaky bits of moss and sod; and while she was thinking of how she'd get across, the old beggar woman appeared to her, but much nicer dressed, touched her shoes with her stick, and the soles spread a foot on each side. So she easily got over the shaky marsh. The burning wood was at the edge of the bog, and there the good fairy flung a damp, thick cloak over her, and through the flames she went, and a hair of her head was not singed. Then they passed through the dark cavern of horrors, where she'd have heard most horrible yells, only that the fairy stopped her ears with wax. She saw frightful things, with blue vapours round them, and felt the sharp rocks, and the slimy backs of frogs and snakes.

When they got out of the cavern, they were at

the mountain of glass; and the fairy made her slippers so sticky with a tap of her rod, that she followed the young corpse easily to the top. There was a deep sea a quarter of a mile under them, and so the corpse said to her, " Go home to my mother, and tell her how far you came to do her bidding : farewell." He sprung head foremost down into the sea, and after him she plunged, without a moment stopping to think about it.

At first she was stupefied, but when they reached the waters she recovered her thoughts, and after piercing down a great depth, she saw a green light towards the bottom. At last they were below the sea, that seemed a green sky above them; and sitting in a beautiful meadow, she half asleep, and her head resting against his side. She couldn't keep her eyes open, and she couldn't tell how long she slept; but when she woke, she was in bed at his house, and he and his mother sitting by her bedside, and watching her.

It was a witch that had a spite to the young man, because he wouldn't marry her, and so she got power to keep him in a state between life and death till a young woman would rescue him by doing as she had just done. So at her request her sisters got their own shape again, and were sent back to their mother, with their spades of gold and shovels of silver. Maybe they were better after that, but I doubt it much. The youngest got the young gentleman for her husband. I'm sure she deserved him, and, if they didn't live happy, THAT WE MAY!

The Brown Bear of Norway

There was once a king in Ireland, and he had three daughters, and very nice princesses they were. And one day that their father and themselves were walking in the lawn, the king began to joke on them, and to ask them who they would like to be married to. "I'll have the King of Ulster for a husband," says one; "and I'll have the King of Munster," says another; "and," says the youngest, "I'll have no husband but the Brown Bear of Norway." For a nurse of her used to be telling her of an enchanted prince that she called by that name, and she fell in love with him, and his name was the first name on her lips, for the very night before she was dreaming of him. Well, one laughed, and another laughed and they joked on the princess all the rest of the evening. But that very night she woke up out of her sleep in a great hall that was lighted with a thousand lamps; the richest carpets were on the floor, and the walls were covered with cloth of gold and silver, and the place was full of grand company, and the very beautiful prince she saw in her dreams was there, and it wasn't a moment till he was on his knees before her, and telling how much he loved, and asking her wouldn't she be his queen. Well, she hadn't the heart to refuse him, and married they were the same evening.

" Now, my darling," says he, when they were left by themselves, "you must know that I'm under enchantment. A sorceress, that had a beautiful daughter, wished me for her son-in-law; and because I didn't keep the young girl at the distance I ought, the mother got power over me, and when I refused to marry her daughter, she made me take the form of a bear by day, and I was to continue so till a lady would marry me of her own free will, and endure five years of great trials after."

Well, when the princess woke in the morning, she missed her husband from her side, and spent the day very sorrowful. But as soon as the lamps were lighted in the grand hall, where she was sitting on a sofa covered with silk, the folding doors flew open and he was sitting by her side the next minute. So they spent another evening so happy, and he took an opportunity of warning her that whenever she began to tire of him, or not to have any confidence in him, they would be parted for ever, and he'd be obliged to marry the witch's daughter.

So she got used to find him absent by day, and they spent a happy twelvemonth together, and at last a beautiful little boy was born; and as happy as she was before, she was twice as happy now, for she had her child to keep her company in the day when she couldn't see her husband.

At last, one evening, when herself, and himself and her child, were sitting with a window open because it was a sultry night, in flew an eagle, took the infant's sash in his beak, and flew up in the air with him. She screamed and was going to throw herself out through the window after him, but the prince caught her, and looked at her very seriously. She thought of what he said soon after their marriage, and she stopped the cries and complaints that were on her lips. She spent her days very lonely for another twelvemonth, when a beautiful little girl was sent to her. Then she thought to herself she'd have a sharp eye about her this time; so she never would allow a window to be more than a few inches open.

But all her care was in vain. Another evening, when they were all so happy, and the prince dandling the baby, a beautiful greyhound bitch stood before them, took the child out of the father's hand, and was out of the door, before you could wink. This time she shouted, and ran out of the room, but there was some of the servants in the next room, and all declared that neither child nor dog passed out. She felt, she could not tell how, to her husband, but still she kept command over herself, and didn't once reproach him.

When the third child was born, she would hardly allow a window or a door to be left open for a moment; but she wasn't the nearer to keep the child to herself. They were sitting one evening by the fire, when a lady appeared standing by them. She opened her eyes in a great fright, and stared at her, and while she was doing so, the appearance wrapped a shawl round the baby that was sitting in its father's lap, and either sunk through the ground with it or went up through the wide chimney. This time the mother kept her bed for a month.

" My dear," said she to her husband, when she was beginning to recover, " I think I'd feel better if I was after seeing my father, and mother, and sisters once more. If you give me leave to go home for a few days, I'd be glad." "Very well," said he, "I will do that; and whenever you feel inclined to return, only mention your wish when you lie down at night." The next morning when she awoke, she found herself in her own old chamber in her father's palace. She rung the bell, and in a short time she had her mother, and father, and married sisters about her, and they laughed till they cried for joy at finding her safe back.

So in time she told them all that happened to her, and they didn't know what to advise her to do. She was as fond of her husband as ever, and she said she was sure that he couldn't help letting the children go; but still she was afraid beyond the world to have another child to be torn from her. Well, the mother and sisters consulted a wise woman that used to bring eggs to the castle, for they had great confidence in her wisdom. She said the only plan was to secure the bear's skin that the prince was obliged to put on every morning, and get it burned, and then he couldn't help being a man night and day, and then the enchantment would be at an end.

So they all persuaded her to do that, and she promised she would; and after eight days she felt so great a longing to see her husband again, that she made the wish the same night, and when she woke three hours after, she was in her husband's palace, and himself was watching over her. There was great joy on both sides, and they were happy for many days.

Now she began to reflect how she never felt her husband leaving her of a morning, and how she never found him neglecting to give her a sweet drink out of a gold cup just as she was going to bed.

So one night she contrived not to drink any of it, though she pretended to do so; and she was awakeful enough in the morning, and saw her husband passing out through a panel in the wainscot, though she kept her eyelids nearly closed. The next night she got a few drops of the sleepy posset that she saved the evening before, put into her husband's night drink, and that made him sleep sound enough. She got up after midnight, passed through the panel, and found a beautiful brown bear's hide hanging in an alcove. She stole back, and went down to the parlour fire, and put the hide into the middle of it, and never took eyes of it till it was all fine ashes. She then lay down by her husband, gave him a kiss on the cheek, and fell asleep.

If she was to live a hundred years, she'd never forget how she wakened next morning, and found her husband looking down on her with misery and anger in his face. " Unhappy woman," said he, " you have separated us for ever! Why hadn't you patience for five years? I am now obliged, whether I like it or not, to go a three days' journey to the witch's castle, and live with her daughter. The skin that was my guard you have burned it, and the egg-wife that gave you the counsel was the witch herself. I won't reproach you: your punishment will be severe enough without it. Farewell for ever!"

He kissed her for the last time, and was off the next minute walking as fast as he could. She shouted after him, and then seeing there was no use, she dressed herself and pursued him. He never stopped, nor stayed, nor looked back, and still she kept him in sight; and when he was on the hill she was in the hollow, and when he was in the hollow she was on the hill. Her life was almost leaving her, when just as the sun was setting, he turned up a bohyeen, and went into a little house. She crawled up after him, and when she got inside there was a beautiful boy on his knees, and he kissing and hugging him. "Here, my poor darling," says he, "is your eldest child, and there," says he, pointing to a nice middle-aged woman that was looking on with a smile on her face, "is the eagle that carried him away." She forgot all her sorrows in a moment, hugging her child, and laughing and crying over him. The Vanithee washed their feet, and rubbed them with an ointment that took all the soreness out of their bones, and made them as fresh as a daisy. Next morning, just before sunrise, he was up and prepared to be off. "Here," said he to her, "is a thing which may be of use to you. It's a scissors, and whatever stuff you cut with it will be turned into rich silk. The moment the sun rises, I'll lose all memory of yourself and the children, but I'll get it at sunset again; farewell." But he wasn't far gone till she was in sight of him again, leaving her boy behind. It was the same to-day as yesterday; their shadows went before them in the morning, and followed them in the evening. He never stopped, and she never stopped, and as the sun was setting, he turned up another lane, and there they found their little daughter. It was all joy and

68

comfort again till morning, and then the third day's journey commenced.

But before he went off, he gave her a comb, and told her that whenever she used it, pearls and diamonds would fall from her hair. Still he had his full memory from sunset to sunrise; but from sunrise to sunset he travelled on under the charm, and never threw his eye behind. This night they came to where the youngest baby was, and the next morning, just before sunrise, the prince spoke to her for the last time. "Here, my poor wife," said he, "is a little hand-reel, with a gold thread that has no end, and the half of our marriage ring. If you can ever get to my bed, put your half ring to mine, I will recollect you. There is a wood yonder, and the moment I enter it, I will forget everything that ever happened between us, as if I was born yesterday. Farewell, dear wife and child, for ever." Just then the sun rose, and away he walked towards the wood. She saw it open before him, and close after him, and when she came up, she could no more get in than she could break through a stone wall. She wrung her hands, and shed tears, but then she recollected herself, and cried out, "Wood, I charge you by my three magic gifts——the scissors, the comb, and the reel—to let me through;" and it opened, and she went along a walk till she came in sight of a palace, and a lawn, and a woodman's cottage in the edge of the wood where it came nearest the palace.

She went into this lodge, and asked the woodman and his wife to take her into their service. They were not willing at first; but she told them she would ask no wages, and would give them diamonds, and pearls, and silk stuffs, and gold threads whenever they wished for them. So they agreed to let her stay.

It wasn't long till she heard how a young prince, that was just arrived, was living in the palace as the husband of the young mistress. Herself and her mother said that they were married fifteen years before, and that he was charmed away from them ever since. He seldom stirred abroad, and every one that saw him remarked how silent and sorrowful he went about, like a person that was searching for some lost thing.

The servants and folks at the big house began to take notice of the beautiful young woman at the lodge, and to annoy her with their impudent addresses. The head-footman was the most troublesome, and at last she invited him to come take tea with her. Oh, how rejoiced he was, and how he bragged of it in the servants' hall! Well, the evening came, and the footman walked into the lodge and was shown to her sitting-room; for the lodge-keeper and his wife stood in great awe of her, and gave her two nice rooms to herself. Well, he sat down as stiff as a ramrod, and was talking in a grand style about the great doings at the castle, while she was getting the tea and toast ready. "Oh," says she to him, "would you put your hand out at the window, and cut me off a sprig or two of honey-suckle?" He got up in great glee, and put out his hand and head; and said she, "By the virtue of my magic gifts, let a pair of horns spring out of your head, and serenade the lodge." Just as she wished, so it was. They sprung from the front of each ear, and tore round the walls till they met at the back. Oh, the poor wretch! and how he bawled and roared! and the servants that he used to be boasting to, were soon flocking from the castle, and grinning, and huzzaing, and beating tunes on tongs, and shovels, and pans; and he cursing and swearing, and the eyes ready to start out of his head, and he so black in his face, and kicking out his legs behind like mad.

At last she pitied his case, and removed the charm, and the horns dropped down on the ground, and he would have killed her on the spot, only he was as weak as water, and his fellow-servants came in, and carried him up to the big house.

Well, some way or other, the story came to the ears of the prince, and he strolled down that way. She had only the dress of a country-woman on her as she sat sewing at the window, but that did not hide her beauty, and he was greatly puzzled, and disturbed, after he had a good look at her features, just as a body is perplexed to know whether something happened to him when he was young, or if he only dreamed it. Well, the witch's daughter heard about it too, and she came to see the strange girl; and what did she find her doing, but cutting out the pattern of a gown from brown paper; and as she cut away, the paper became the richest silk she ever saw. The lady looked on with very covetous eyes, and says she, " What would you be satisfied to take for that scissors?" " I'll take nothing," says she, " but leave to spend one night in the prince's chamber, and I'll swear to be as innocent of any crime next morning as we were in the evening." Well, the proud lady fired up, and was going to say something dreadful; but the scissors kept on cutting, and the silk growing richer and richer every inch. So she agreed, and made her take a great oath to keep her promise.

When night came on she was let into her husband's chamber, and the door was locked. But, when she came in a tremble, and sat by the bedside, the prince was in such a dead sleep, that all she did couldn't wake him. She sung this verse to him, sighing and sobbing, and kept singing it the night long, and it was all in vain:

" Four long years I was married to thee;
Three sweet babes I bore to thee;
Brown Bear of Norway, won't you turn to me?"

At the first dawn, the proud lady was in the chamber, and led her away, and the footman of the horns put out his tongue at her as she was quitting the palace.

So there was no luck so far; but the next day the prince passed by again, and looked at her and saluted her kindly, as a prince might a farmer's daughter, and passed on; and soon the witch's daughter came by, and found her combing her hair, and pearls and diamonds dropping from it.

Well, another bargain was made, and the princess spent another night of sorrow, and she left the castle at daybreak, and the footman was at his post, and enjoyed his revenge.

The third day the prince went by, and stopped to talk with the strange woman. He asked her could he do anything to serve her, and she said he might. She asked him did he ever wake at night.

He said that he was rather wakeful than other-wise; but that during the last two nights, he was listening to a sweet song in his dreams, and could not wake, and that the voice was one that he must have known and loved in some other world long ago. Says she, " Did you drink any sleepy posset either of these evenings before you went to bed?" " I did," said he. " The two evenings my wife gave me something to drink, but I don't know whether it was a sleepy posset or not." " Well, prince," said she, " as you say you would wish to oblige me, you can do it by not tasting any drink this afternoon." " I will not," says he, and then he went on his walk.

Well, the great lady came soon after the prince, and found the stranger using her hand-reel and winding threads of gold off, and the third bargain was made.

That evening the prince was lying on his bed at twilight, and his mind much disturbed; and the door opened, and in his princess walked, and down she sat by his bed-side, and sung:—

" Four long years I was married to thee;
    Three sweet babies I bore to thee;
    Brown Bear of Norway, won't you turn to
        me?"

" Brown Bear of Norway!" said he. " I don't understand you." " Don't you remember, prince, that I was your wedded wife for four years?" " I do not," said he, " but I'm sure I wish it was so." " Don't you remember our three babies, that are still alive?" " Show me them. My mind is all a

73

heap of confusion." " Look for the half of our marriage ring, that hangs at your neck, and fit it to this." He did so, and the same moment the charm was broken. His full memory came back on him, and he flung his arms round his wife's neck, and both burst into tears.

Well, there was a great cry outside, and the castle walls were heard splitting and cracking. Every one in the castle was alarmed, and made their way out. The prince and princess went with the rest, and by the time all were safe on the lawn, down came the building, and made the ground tremble for miles round. No one ever saw the witch and her daughter afterwards. It was not long till the prince and princess had their children with them, and then they set out for their own palace. The kings of Ireland, and of Munster and Ulster, and their wives, soon came to visit them, and may every one that deserves it be as happy as the Brown Bear of Norway and his family.

The Goban Saor

It is a long time since the Goban Saor was alive. Maybe it was him that built the Castle of Ferns; part of the walls are thick enough to be built by any goban, or gow, that ever splintered wood, or hammered red-hot iron, or cut a stone. If he didn't build Ferns, he built other castles for some of the five kings or the great chiefs. He could fashion a spear-shaft while you'd count five, and the spear-head at three strokes of a hammer. When he wanted to drive big nails into beams that were ever so high from the ground, he would pitch them into their place, and, taking a fling of the hammer at their heads, they would be drove in as firm as the knocker of Newgate, and he would catch the hammer when it was falling down.

At last it came to the King of Munster's turn to get his castle built, and to Goban he sent. Goban knew that, in other times far back, the King of Ireland killed the celebrated architects, Rog, Robog, Rodin, and Rooney, the way they would never build another palace equal to his, and so he mentioned something to his wife privately before he set out. He took his son along with him, and the first night they lodged at a farmer's house. The farmer told them they might leave their beasts to graze all night in any of his fields they pleased. So they entered one field, and says Goban, "Tie the bastes up for the night." "Why?" says the son; "I can't find anything strong enough." "Well, then, let us try the next field. Now," says he, "tie up the horses if you can." "Oh! by my word, here's a thistle strong enough this time." "That will do."

The next night they slept at another farmer's house, where there were two young daughters—one with black hair, very industrious; the other with fair complexion, and rather liking to sit with her hands across, and listen to the talk round the fire, than to be doing any work. While they were chatting about one thing and another, says the

Goban, "Young girls, if I'd wish to be young again, it would be for the sake of getting one of you for a wife; but I think very few old people that do be thinking at all of the other world, ever wish to live their lives over again. Still I wish that you may have good luck in your choice of a husband, and so I give you three bits of advice. Always have the head of an old woman by the hob; warm yourselves with your work in the morning; and some time before I come back, take the skin of a newly-killed sheep to the market, and bring itself and the price of it home again." When they were leaving next morning, the Goban said to his son, " Maybe one of these girls may be your wife some day."

As they were going along, they met a poor man striving to put a flat roof over a mud-walled round cabin, but he had only three joists, and each of them was only three quarters of the breadth across. Well, the Goban put two nicks near one end of every joist on opposite sides; and when these were fitted into one another, there was a three-cornered figure formed in the middle, and the other ends rested on the mud wall, and the floor they made was as strong as anything. The poor man blessed the two men, and they went on. That night they stopped at a house where the master sat by the fire, and hardly opened his mouth all evening. If he didn't talk, a meddlesome neighbour did, and interfered about everything. There was another chance lodger besides the Goban and his son, and when the evening was half over, the Goban said he thought he would go farther on his journey as it was a fine night. " You may come along with us, if you like," says he to the other man; but he said he was too tired. The two men slept in a farmer's house half a mile farther on; and the next morning the first news they heard, when they were setting out, was that the man of the house they left the evening before was found murdered in his bed, and the lodger taken up on suspicion. Says he to his son, " Never sleep a night where the woman is everything and the man nothing." He stopped a day or two, however, and by cross-examining and calling witnesses, he got the murder tracked to the woman and the busy neighbour.

The next day they came to a ford, where a dozen of carpenters were puzzling their heads about setting up a wooden bridge that would neither have a peg nor a nail in any part of it. The king would give a great reward to them if they succeeded, and if they didn't, he'd never give one of them a job again. " Give us a hatchet and a few sticks," says the Goban, " and we'll see if we have any little genius that way." So he squared a few posts and cross-bars, and made a little bridge on the sod; and it was so made, that the greater weight was on it, and the stronger the stream of water, the solider it would be.

Maybe the carpenters warn't thankful, except one envious, little, ould basthard of a fellow, that said any child might have thought of the plan (it happened he didn't think of it though), and he would make the Goban and his son drink a cag of whisky, only they couldn't delay their journey.

At last they came to where the King of Munster kep' his coort, either at Cashel or Limerick, or some place in Clare, and the Goban burned very little daylight till he had a palace springing up like a flagger. People came from all parts, and were in admiration of the fine work; but as they were getting near the eaves, one of the carpenters that were engaged at the wooden bridge came late one night into the Goban's room, and told him what himself was suspecting, that just as he would be setting the coping stone, the scaffolding would, somehow or other, get loose, himself fall down a few stories and be kilt, the king wring his hands, and shed a few crocodile tears, and the like palace never be seen within the four seas of Ireland.

"*Sha gu dheine*," says the Goban to himself; but next day he spoke out plain enough to the king. "Please your Majesty," says he, "I am now pretty near the end of my work, but there is still something to be done before we come to the wall-plate that is to make all sure and strong. There is a bit of charm about it, and I haven't the tool here—it is at home, and my son got so sick last night, and is lying so bad, he is not able to go for it. If you can't spare the young prince, I must go myself, for my wife wouldn't intrust it to any one but of royal blood." The king, rather than let the Goban out of his sight, sent the young prince for the tool. The Goban told him some outlandish name in Irish, which his wife would find at his bed's head, and bid him make all the haste he could back.

In a week's time, back came two of the poor attendants that were with the prince, and told the king that his son was well off, the best of eating and drinking, and chess-playing and sword exer-

78

cise, 'that any prince could wish for, but that out
of her sight the Goban's wife nor her people would
let him, till she had her husband safe and sound
inside of his own threshold.

Well, to be sure, how the king fumed and raged!
but what's the use of striving to tear down a stone
wall with your teeth? He could do without his
palace being finished, but he couldn't without his
son and heir. The Goban didn't keep spite; he put
the finishing touch to the palace in three days, and,
in two days more, himself and his son were sitting
at the farmer's fireside where the two purty young
girls wor.

"Well, my colleen bawn," says he to the one
with the fair hair, "did you mind the advice I
gev you when I was here last?" "Indeed I did, and
little good it did me. I got an old woman's skull
from the churchyard, and fixed it in the wall near
the hob, and it so frightened every one, that I was
obliged to have taken it back in an hour." "And
how did you warm yourself with your work in the
cold mornings?" "The first morning's work I had
to card flax, and I thrune some of it on the fire,
and my mother gave me such a raking for it, that
I didn't offer to warm myself that way again."
"Now for the sheep-skin." "That was the worst of
all. When I told the buyers in the market that I
was to bring hack the skin and the price of it,
they only jeered at me. One young buckeen said,
if I'd go into the tavern and take share of a quart
of mulled beer with him, he'd make that bargain
with me, and that so vexed me that I turned home
at once." "Well, that was the right thing to do,
anyhow. Now my little Ceann Dhu, let us see how

you fared. The skull?" "Och!" says an old woman, sitting close to the fire in the far corner, " I'm a distant relation that was desolate, and this," says she, tapping the side of her poor head, " is the old woman's skull she provided." " Well, now for the warming of yourself in the cold mornings." " Oh, I kept my hands and feet going so lively at my work that it was warming enough." " Well, and the sheep-skin?" " That was easy enough. When I got to the market, I went to the crane, plucked the wool off, sold it, and brought home the skin."

" Man and woman of the house," says the Goban, " I ask you before this company, to give me this girl for my daughter-in-law; and if ever her husband looks crooked at her, I'll beat him within an inch of his life." There was very few words, and no need of a black man to make up the match; and when the prince was returning home, he stopped a day to be at the wedding. If I hear of any more of the Goban's great doings, I'll tell them some other time.

The Grateful Beasts

There was once a young man, and it happened that he had a guinea in his pocket, and was going to some fair or pattern or another, and while he was on the way, he saw some little boys scourging a poor mouse they were after catching. " Come, gorsoons," says he, " don't be at that cruel work:

here's sixpence for you to buy gingerbread and let him go." They only wanted the wind of the word, and off jumped the mouse. He didn't go much farther when he overtook another parcel of young *geochachs,* and they tormenting the life out of a poor weasel. Well, he bought him off for a shilling, and went on. The third creature he rescued from a crowd of grown up young rascals was an ass, and he had to give a whole half crown to get him off.

"Now," says poor Neddy, "you may as well take me with you. I'll be of some use carrying you when you're tired." "With all my heart," says Jack. The day was very hot, and the boy sat under a tree to enjoy the cool. As sure as he did he fell asleep without intending it, but he was soon woke up by a wicked looking *bodach* and his two servants. "How dare you let your ass go trespass on my inch," says he to Jack, "and do such mischief." "I had no notion he'd do anything of the kind : I dropped asleep by accidence." "Oh be this an' be that ! I'll accidence you. Bring out that chest," says he to one of his giollas; and while you'd be sayin' thrapsticks they had the poor boy lyin' on the broad of his back in it, and a strong hempen rope tied round it, and himself an' itself flung into the river.

Well, they went away to their business, and poor Neddy stayed roarin' an' bawlin' on the bank, till who should come up but the weasel and the mouse, and they axed him what ailed him. "An' isn't the kind boy that rescued me from them scoggins that were tormenting me just now, fastened up in a chest and drivin down that terrible river?" "Oh," says the weasel, "he must be the same boy that rescued the mouse and myself. Had he a brown piece on the elbow of his coat?" "The very same." "Come then," says the weasel, "and let us overtake him, and get him out." "By all means," says the others. So the weasel got on the ass's back, and the mouse in his ear, and away with them. They hadn't the trouble of going far, when they see the chest which was stopped among the rushes at the edge of a little island. Over they went, and the weasel and the mouse gnawed the rope till they had the led off, and their master out on the bank. Well, they were all very glad, and were conversing together, when what should the weasel spy but a beautiful egg with the loveliest colours on the shell lying down in the shallow water? He wasn't long till he had it up, and Jack was turning it round and round, and admiring it. "Oh, musha, my good friends," says he, "I wish it was in my power to show my gratitude to you, and that I had a fine castle and estate where we could live with full and plenty!" The words were hardly out of his mouth when the beasts and himself found themselves standing on the steps of a castle, and the finest lawn before it that ever you saw.

There was no one inside nor outside to dispute possession with them, and there they lived as happy as kings. They found money enough inside a cupboard, and the house had the finest furniture in every room, and it was an easy matter to hire servants and labourers.

Jack was standing at his gate one day, as three merchants were passing by with their goods packed on the backs of horses and mules. "Death alive!" says they, "what's this for? There was neither castle, nor lawn, nor three here the last time we went by."

"True for you!" says Jack. "But you shan't be the worse for it. Take your beasts into the bawn behind the house, and give 'em a good feed, and if you're not in a hurry, stay and take a bit of dinner with myself." They wished for no better, and after dinner the innocent slob of a Jack let himself be overtaken, and showed them his painted egg, and told 'em everything that happened him. As sure as the hearth money, one of 'em puts a powder in Jack's next tumbler, and when he woke it was in the island he found himself, with his patched coat on him, and his three friends sitting on their *currabingoes* near him, and looking very down in the mouth.

"Ah master!" says the weasel, " you'll never be wise enough for the tricky people that's in the world. Where did them thieves say they lived, and what's the name that's on 'em?" Jack scratched his head, and after a little recollected the town. "Come, Neddy," says the weasel, " let us be jogging." So he got on his back, and the mouse in his ear, and the ass swum the river, and nothing is said of their travels till they came to the house of the head rogue. The mouse went in, and the ass and the weasel sheltered themselves in a copse outside. He soon came back to them. " Well, what news?" " Dull news enough. He has the egg in a low press in his bedroom, and a pair of cats with fiery eyes watching it night and day, and they chained to the press, and the room door double locked." " Let us go back!" says the ass; " we can't do nothing." " Wait," says the weasel.

When sleep time came. says the weasel to the mouse, " Go in at the key hole, and get behind the rogue's head, an' stay two or three hours sucking his hair." " What good in that?" says the ass. " Wait, an' you'll know," says the weasel. Next morning the merchant was quite mad to find the way his hair was in. " But I'll disappoint you tonight, you thief of a mouse," says he. So he unchained the cats next night, and bid them sit by his bedside and watch.

Just as he was dropping asleep, the weasel and mouse were outside the door, and gnawing away till they had a hole scooped out at the bottom. In went the mouse, and it wasn't long till he had the egg outside. They were soon on the road again; the mouse in the ass's ear, the weasel on his back, and the egg in the weasel's mouth. When they came to the river, and were swimming across, the ass began to bray. " Hee haw, hee haw!" says he, " is there the likes of me in the world? I'm carrying the mouse, and the weasel, and the great enchanted egg, that can do anything. Why don't yous praise me?" But the mouse was asleep, and the weasel was afraid of opening his mouth. " I'll shake yous off, you ungrateful pack if you don't," says the ass again; and the poor weasel, forgetting himself, cried out, " Oh, don't!" and down went the egg in the deepest pool of the river. " Now you done it," says the weasel, and you may be sure the ass looked very lewd of himself. " Oh, what are we to do now, at all, at all?" says he. " Never despair," says the weasel. He looked down into the deep water and cried, " Hear, all you frogs and fish! There is a great army coming to take yous

84

out, and eat yous red raw; look sharp!" "Oh, and what can we do?" says they, coming up to the top. "Gather up all the stones, and hand them to us, and we'll make a big wall on the bank to defend you." They began to work like little divels in a mud wall, and were hard and fast reaching up the pebbles they found on the bottom. At last a big frog came up with the egg in his mouth, and when the weasel had hold of it, he got up in a tree, and cried out, "That will do. The army is frightened and running away." So the poor things were greatly relieved.

You may be sure that Jack was very rejoiced to see his friends and the egg again. They were soon back in their castle and lawn, and when Jack began to feel lonesome he did not find it hard to make out a fine young wife for himself, and his three friends were as happy as the day was long.

The Lazy Beauty and Her Aunts

There was once a poor widow woman, who had a daughter that was as handsome as the day, and as lazy as a pig, saving your presence. The poor mother was the most industrious person in the townland, and was a particularly good hand at the spinning-wheel. It was the wish of her heart that her daughter should be as handy as herself; but she'd get up late, eat her breakfast before she'd finish her prayers, and then go about dawdling, and anything she handled seemed to be burning her fingers. She drawled her words as if it was a great trouble to her to speak, or as if her tongue was as lazy as her body. Many a heart-scold her poor mother got with her, and still she was only improving like dead fowl in August.

Well, one morning when things were as bad as they could be, and the poor woman was giving tongue at the rate of a mill-clapper, who should be riding by but the king's son. "Oh dear, oh dear, good woman!" said he, " you must have a very bad child to make you scold so terribly. Sure it can't be this handsome girl that vexed you!" " Oh, please your Majesty, not at all," says the old dissembler. " I was only checking her for working herself too much. Would your Majesty believe it? She spins three pounds of flax in a day, weaves it into linen the next, and makes it all into shirts the day after." " My gracious," says the prince, " she's the very lady that will just fill my mother's eye, and herself the greatest spinner in the kingdom. Will you put on your daughter's bonnet and cloak if you please, ma'am, and set her behind me? Why, my mother will be so delighted with her, that perhaps she'll make her her daughter-in-law in a week, that is, if the young woman herself is agreeable."

Well, between the confusion, and the joy, and the fear of being found out, the woman didn't know what to do; and before they could make up their minds, young handsome Anty was set behind the prince, and away he and his attendants went, and a good heavy purse was left behind with the mother. She *pullillued* a long time after all was gone, in dread of something bad happening to the poor girl.

The prince couldn't judge of the girl's breeding or wit from the few answers he pulled out of her. The queen was struck in a heap when she saw a young country girl sitting behind her son, but when she saw her handsome face, and heard all she could do, she didn't think she could make too much of her. The prince took an opportunity of whispering her that if she didn't object to be his wife she must strive to please his mother. Well, the evening went by, and the prince and Anty were getting fonder and fonder of one another, but the thought of the spinning used to send the cold to her heart every moment. When bed-time came, the old queen went along with her to a beautiful bedroom, and when she was bidding her good-night, she pointed to a heap of fine flax, and said, " You may begin as soon as you like to-morrow morning, and I'll expect to see these three pounds in nice thread the morning after." Little did the poor girl sleep that night. She kept crying and lamenting that she didn't mind her mother's advice better. When she was left alone next morning, she began with a heavy heart; and though she had a nice mahogany wheel and the finest flax you ever saw, the thread was breaking every moment. One while it was as fine as a cobweb, and the next as coarse as a little boy's whipcord. At last she pushed her chair back, let her hands fall in her lap, and burst out a-crying.

A small old woman with surprising big feet appeared before her the same moment, and said, " What ails you, you handsome colleen?" " An' haven't I all that flax to spin before to-morrow morning, and I'll never be able to have even five yards of fine thread of it put together." " An'

87

would you think bad to ask poor Colliach Cushmor
with the big foot to your wedding with the young
prince? If you promise me that, all your three
pounds will be made into the finest of thread
while you're taking your sleep to-night." "Indeed
you must be there and welcome, and I'll honour
you all the days of your life." "Very well; stay in
your room till tea-time and tell the queen she may
come in for her thread as early as she likes to-
morrow morning." It was all as she said; and the
thread was finer and evener than the gut you see
with fly-fishers. "My brave girl you were," says the
queen. "I'll get my own mahogany loom brought
into you, but you needn't do anything more to-
day. Work and rest, work and rest, is my motto.
To-morrow you'll weave all this thread, and who
knows what may happen?"

The poor girl was more frightened this time than
the last, and she was so afraid to lose the prince.

She didn't even know how to put the warp in
the gears, nor how to use the shuttle, and she was
sitting in the greatest grief, when a little woman
who was mighty well-shouldered about the hips all
at once appeared to her, told her her name was
Colliach Cromanmor, and made the same bargain
with her as Colliach Cushmor. Great was the
queen's pleasure when she found early in the morning a web as fine and white as the finest paper you
ever saw. "The darling you were!" says she.
"Take your ease with the ladies and gentlemen
to-day, and if you have all this made into nice shirts
to-morrow you may present one of them to my
son, and be married to him out of hand."

Oh, wouldn't you pity poor Anty the next day,

she was now so near the prince, and, maybe, would be soon so far from him. But she waited as patiently as she could with scissors, needle, and thread in hand, till a minute after noon. Then she was rejoiced to see the third old woman appear. She had a big red nose, and informed Anty that people called her Shron Mor Rua on that account. She was up to her as good as the others, for a dozen shirts were lying on the table when the queen paid her an early visit.

Now there was nothing talked of but the wedding, and I needn't tell you it was grand. The poor mother was there along with the rest, and at the dinner the old queen could talk of nothing but the lovely shirts, and how happy herself and the bride would be after the honeymoon, spinning, and weaving, and sewing shirts and shirts without end. The bridegroom didn't like the discourse, and the bride liked it less, and he was going to say something, when the footman came up to the head of the table, and said to the bride, " Your ladyship's aunt, Colliach Cushmor, bade me ask might she come in." The bride blushed and wished she was seven miles under the floor, but well became the prince—" Tell Mrs. Cushmor," said he, " that any relation of my bride's will be always heartily welcome wherever she and I are." In came the woman with the big foot, and got a seat near the prince. The old queen didn't like it much, and after a few words she asked rather spitefully, " Dear ma'am, what's the reason your foot is so big?" " Musha, faith, your majesty, I was standing almost all my life at the spinning-wheel, and that's the reason." " I declare to you, my darling," said the prince,

" I'll never allow you to spend one hour at the same spinning-wheel." The same footman said again, " Your ladyship's aunt, Colliach Croman-mor, wishes to come in, if the genteels and yourself have no objection." Very displeased was Princess Anty, but the prince sent her welcome, and she took her seat, and drank healths apiece to the company. " May I ask, ma'am?" says the old queen, " why you're so wide half-way between the head and the feet?" " That, your majesty, is owing to sitting all my life at the loom." " By my sceptre," says the prince, " my wife shall never sit there an hour." The footman came up again. " Your lady-ship's aunt, Colliach Shron Mor Rua, is asking leave to come into the banquet." More blushing on the bride's face, but the bridegroom spoke out cordially, " Tell Mrs. Shron Mor Rua she's doing us an honour." In came the old woman, and great respect she got near the top of the table, but the people down low put up their tumblers and glasses to their noses to hide the grins. " Ma'am," says the old queen, " will you tell us, if you please, why your nose is so big and red?" " Troth, your majesty, my head was bent down over the stitch-ing all my life, and all the blood in my body ran into my nose." " My darling," said the prince to Anty, " if ever I see a needle in your hand, I'll run a hundred miles from you."

And in troth, girls and boys, though it's a diverting story, I don't think the moral is good; and if any of you thuckeens go about imitating Anty in her laziness, you'll find it won't thrive with you as it did with her. She was beautiful beyond compare, which none of you are, and she had three powerful fairies to help her besides. There's no fairies now, and no prince or lord to ride by, and catch you idling or working; and maybe, after all, the prince and herself were not so very happy when the cares of the world or old age came on them.

Hairy Rouchy

There was once a widow woman, as often there was, and she had three daughters. The eldest and the second eldest were as handsome as the moon and the evening star, but the youngest was all covered with hair, and her face was as brown as a berry, and they called her Hairy Rouchy. She lighted the fire in the morning, cooked the food, and made the beds, while her sisters would be stringing flowers on a hank, or looking at themselves in the glass, or sitting with their hands across. "No one will ever come to marry us in this lonesome place," said the eldest, one day; "so you and I," said she to the second sister, "may as well go seek our fortune." "That's the best word you ever spoke," said the other. "Bake our cake and kill our cock, mother, and away we go." Well, so she did. "And now, girls," said she, "which will you have, half this with my blessing, or the whole of it with my curse?" "Curse or no curse, mother, the whole of it is little enough."

Well, they set off, and says Hairy Rouchy to her mother when they got to the end of the lane, "Mother, give me your blessing, and a quarter of the griddle cake, I must go after these girls, for I fear ill luck is in their road." She gave her blessing and the whole of the cake, and she went off running, and soon overtook them. "Here's Hairy Rouchy," says the eldest, "she'll make a show of us. We'll tie her to this big stone." So they tied her to the big stone and went their way, but when they were a quarter of a mile further, there she was three perches behind them. Well, they were vexed enough, and the next clamp of turf they passed, they made her lie down, and piled every sod of it over her.

When they were a quarter of a mile further they looked back again, and there was the girl three perches behind them, and weren't they mad! To make a long story short, they fastened her in a pound, and they put the tying of the three smalls on her, and fastened her to a tree. The next quarter of a mile she was up by their side, and at last they were tired, and let her walk behind them.

Well, they walked and they walked till they were tired, and till the greyness of night came round them, and they saw a light at a distance. When they came up, what was it but a giant's house, and great sharp teeth were in the heads of himself, and his wife, and his three daughters. Well, they got lodging, and when sleep time was coming they were put into one bed, and the giant's daughters' bed touched the head of theirs. Well becomes my brave Hairy Rouchy, when the giant's daughters were asleep, she took off the hair necklaces from her own neck and the necks of her sisters, and put them on the giant's daughters' necks, and she put their gold and silver and diamond necklaces on the necks of her sisters and herself, and then watched to see what would happen.

The giant and his wife were sitting by the fire, and says he, " Won't these girls make a fine meat pie for us to-morrow." " Won't they," says she, and she smacked her lips, " but I'll have some trouble singeing that hairy one ". " They are all asleep now," says he, and he called in his red-headed giolla. " Go and put them strangers out of pain," says he. " But how'll I know them from your daughters," says the giolla. " Very easy, they have only hair necklaces round their necks."

Well, you may all guess what happened. So the night faded away, and the morning came, and what did the giant see at the flight of darkness, when the gate was opened by the cow-boy, but Hairy Rouchy walking out through it after her two sisters. Down the stairs he came, five at a time, and out of the bawn he flew, and *magh go bragh* with him after the girls. The eldest screamed out, and the second eldest screamed out, but the youngest took one under each arm, and if she didn't lay leg to ground, you may call me a story-teller. She ran like the wind, and the giant ran like the north wind; the sparks of fire he struck out of the stones hit her on the back, and the sparks of fire she struck out of the stones scorched his face. At last they came near the wide and deep river that divided his land from the land of the King of Spain, and into that land he daren't pass. Over the wide deep river went Hairy Rouchy with a high, very active bound, and after her went the giant. His heels touched the bank, and back into the water went his head and body. He dragged himself out on his own side, and sat down on the bank, and looked across, and this is what he said: " You're there, Hairy Rouchy," says he. " No thanks to you for it," says she. " You got my three daughters killed," says he. " It was to save our own lives," says she. " When will you come to see me again," says he. " When I have business," says she. " Divel be in your road," says he. " It's better pray than curse," says she.

The three girls went on till they came to the King of Spain's castle, where they were well enter- tained, and the King's eldest son and the eldest sister fell in love with one another, and the second son and the second sister fell in love with one another, and poor Hairy Rouchy fell in love with the youngest son, but he didn't fall in love with her.

Well, the next day, when they were at breakfast, says the King to her, " Good was your deed at the giant's house, and if you only bring me the talking golden quilt that's covering himself and his wife, my eldest son may marry your eldest sister." " I'll try," says she, " worse than lose I can't."

So that night, when the giant and his wife were fast asleep, the quilt felt a hand pulling it off the bed. " Who are you?" says the quilt. " Mishe " (myself), says the girl, and she pulled away. " Waken, master," says the quilt, " some one is taking me away." " And who's taking you away?" says he. " It's Mishe that's doing it," says the quilt. " Then let Mishe stop his tricks, and not

94

be disturbing us." "But I tell you, Mishe is carrying me off." "If Mishe says another word, I'll get up and throw him in the fire." So the poor quilt had nothing to do but hold its tongue.

"But," says the giant's wife, after a few minutes, "maybe the divel bewitched the quilt to walk off with itself." "Faith and maybe so," says the giant; "I'll get up and look." So he searched the room, and the stairs, and the hall, and the bawn, and the bawn gate was open. "*Mile mollachd*," says he; "Hairy Rouchy was here," and to the road he took. But when he was on the hill she was in the hollow, and when he was in the hollow she was on the hill, and when he came to the hither side of the river she was on the thither. "You're there, Hairy Rouchy," says he. "No thanks to you," says she. "You took away my speaking golden quilt," says he. "It was to get my eldest sister married," says she. "When will you come again?" "Divel be in your road," says he. "It's better pray than curse," says she; and the same night the speaking golden quilt was covering the King and Queen of Spain.

Well, the wedding was made, but there was little notice taken of poor Hairy Rouchy, and she spent a good part of the day talking to a poor travelling woman that she often relieved at home and that was come by accident as far as Spain.

So the next day, when they were at breakfast again, says the King, "Hairy Rouchy, if you bring me tomorrow morning the *chloive solais* that hangs at the giant's bed's head, my second son will marry your second sister." "I'll make the trial," says she; "worse than lose I can't."

Well, the next night the giant's wife was boiling his big pot of gruel, and Hairy Rouchy was sitting by the chimbly on the scraws that covered the ridge pole, and dropping fistfuls of salt into the pot. "You put too much salt in this porridge," says the giant to his wife, when he was supping it. "I'm sure I didn't put in more than four spoonfuls," says she. "Well, well, that was the right size; still it tastes mortial salty."

When he was in bed he cried out, "Wife, I'll be a piece of cured bacon before morning if I don't get a drink." "Oh, then, purshuin to the sup of water in the house," says she. "Well, call up the giolla out of the settle, and let him bring a pailful from the well." So the giolla got up in a bad humour, scratching his head, and went to the door with the pail in his hand. There was Hairy Rouchy by the jamb, and maybe she didn't dash fistfuls of sand and salt into his eyes. "Oh, master, master," says he, "the sky is as black as your hat, and it's pelting hailstones on me; I'll never find the well." "Here you *onshuch,* take the sword of light, and it will show you the way."

So he took the *chloive solais,* and made his way to the well, and while he was filling the pail he laid the sword on the ground. That was all the girl wanted. She snatched it up, waved it round her head, and the light flashed over hills and hollows. "If you're not into the house like a shot," says she, "I'll send your head half a mile away." The poor giolla was only too glad to get off, and she was soon flying like the wind to the river, and the giant hot foot after her. When she was in the hollow he was on the hill. . . .

96

"You're a very good girl, indeed," says the King of Spain to Hairy Rouchy, the morning after the second marriage. "You deserve a reward. So bring me the giant's puckawn with the golden bells round his neck as soon as you like, and you must get my youngest son for a husband." "But maybe he won't have me," says she. "Indeed an' I will," says the prince; "so good a sister can't make a bad wife." "But I'm all hairy and brown," says she. "That's no sin," says the prince.

Sure enough, the night after, she was hard and fast in the giant's outhouse, stuffing the puckawn's bells with the marrow of the elder; and when she thought the job was well finished she was leading him out. She had a band on his mouth, but when my brave puck found he couldn't bawl, he took to rear and kick like a puck as he was. Out came the elder marrow from three of the bells, and the sound that came from them was enough to waken the dead. She drove him at his full speed before her, but after came the giant like a storm. She could escape him if she liked, but she would not return without puck, and bedad she was soon pinned and brought back to the giant's big kitchen. There was his wife and the giolla, and if he wasn't proud to show them his prisoner there's not a glove in Wexford.

"Now, ma'am," says he to her, "I have you safe after all the mischief you done me. If I was in your power what would you do to me?" "Oh, wouldn't I tie you up to the ceiling in a sack, you ould tyrant, and go myself and giolla to the wood, cut big clubs, and break every bone in your body one after another. Then if there was any life left

97

D

in you, we'd make a fire of the green boughs underneath, and stifle the little that was left out of you." " The very thing I'll do with you," says he.

So he put her in a sack, tied her up to the beam that went across the kitchen, and went off with the giolla to the wood to cut down the clubs and green branches, leaving his wife to watch the prisoner. She expected to hear crying and sobbing from out of the sack, but the girl did nothing but shout and laugh. " Is it mad, you are," says she, " and death so near you?" " Death indeed. Why, the bottom of the sack is full of diamonds, and pearls, and guineas, and there is the finest views all round me you ever see—castles, and lawns, and lakes, and the finest flowers." " Is it lies you're telling?" " Oh, dickens a lie. If I'd let you up, but I won't, you'd see and feel it all."

But the giant's wife over-persuaded her, and when she was loosened, and got the other into the sack, she tied her hard and fast, ran to the out-house, threw a rope round the puckawn's neck, and he and she were soon racing like the wind to-ward the river. The giant and the giolla were soon back, and he wondered where his wife could be. But he saw the sack still full, and the two began to whack it like so many blacksmiths. " Oh, Lord," says the poor woman, " it's myself that's here." But she roared out, "Ah, sure, I'm your wife, don't kill me for goodness's sake." " Be the laws," says the giolla, " it's the mistress. Oh, bad luck to you, Hairy Rouchy; this is your doing. Run and catch her, master, while I take the poor mistress down, and see what I can do for her." Off went the big fellow like a bowarra, but when he came to this

98

side of the river panting and puffing, there was the girl and his darling puckawn on the other side, and she ready to burst her sides with the laughing.

"You're there, my damsel." "No thanks, etc." So the scolding match went on to the end and then says he, "If you were in my place and I in yours now, what would you do?" "I'd stoop down and drink the river dry to get at you." But she didn't stop to see whether he was fool enough to take her advice, but led her goat to the palace. Oh, wasn't there great joy and clapping of hands when the golden bells were heard a-ringing up the avenue, and into the big bawn. She didn't mind how any one looked but the youngest prince; and though he didn't appear very rejoiced, there was a kind of smile in his face, and she was satisfied.

Well, the next morning, when they were all setting out to the church, and the bridegroom was mounted on his horse, and the bride getting into the coach, she asked him for leave to take the poor travelling woman in along with her. "It's a queer request," says he, "but do as you like; you must have some reason for it." Well, when all were dismounting or getting out of their coaches, he went to open the door for his bride, and the sight almost left his eyes; for there sitting fornent him was the most beautiful young woman he ever beheld. She had the same kind innocent look that belonged to Hairy Rouchy, but she had also the finest colour in her face, and neck, and hands, and her hair, instead of the tangled brake it used to be, was nicely platted and curled, and was the finest dark brown in the world.

Glad enough she was to see the joy and surprise

in his face, and if they were not the happy bride
and bridegroom I never saw one. When they were
talking by themselves, she told him that an enchantment was laid on her when she was a child,
and she was always to remain the fright she was,
till someone would marry her for the sake of her
disposition. The travelling woman was her guar-
dian fairy in disguise. There were two unhappy
marriages and one happy one in the King of
Spain's family, and I'll let every one here guess
which was which.

The Wise Men of Gotham

There was once a townland called Gotham, but
maybe it's now swallowed up and covered with
sand like Bannow, or maybe a moving bog went
over it, for I never heard any one say he knew
where it was. Well, four brothers lived in it, and
they were called the wise men of Gotham, and
you might as well call Pat Neil a wise man, I'm
sure. One of them took a big cheese to town to
sell it one market day. He was on horseback, and
just as he came to the brow of a steep hill just
outside the town, the cheese dropped and began
to roll down the slope like vengeance. " Oh, no!"
says he, " is that the way! I'll take this other road
into town, and I'll engage I'll get there before
100

you." So he put spurs to his horse, and he was soon in the nighest street that was just at the bottom of the hill. Neither the cheese nor the ghost of the cheese was there. He rode up the hill, and looked in the dykes for his cheese, but, 'deed, he returned home hungry and dry, and he had neither the cheese nor the value of it.

Well, they were blaming him, sure enough, till he began to think he hadn't done a very wise thing after all. "And what would you do if you were in my place?" said he to one of his brothers. "Well, I think I'd go and buy another cheese the same size and roll it down, and ride after it and see where it would go." "That's not a bad thought," says another, "but if it happened to me I think I'd sit at the market-cross till I'd hear the bell-man crying out where it was to be got, for it's very likely some honest man found it." "But," says the last, "I think I'd pay Bowzy, the bellman of Enniscorthy, a thirteen to cry it, and offer half of it for reward. For didn't yez all often hear, 'Half a loaf is better than no bread'?"

Next market day another of the brothers went to sell another cheese, and he determined he'd be very cunning if any mischance happened him. Well, just at the very same place he dropped his cheese too. It didn't roll, for it came down in a car-track. This second wise man pulled out his sword, and made a prod at it to lift it up, but it was too short, and if it was long enough itself, it was too blunt at the end. So he rode into the town and bought a long sword with a sharp point at the cutler's, and rode back again.

His cheese wasn't there, nor half way down the

101

hill, nor at the bottom of the hill. He recollected
what was said at home, and sat at the market
cross till sunset to see if the honest finder would
cry it. Then he paid his thirteen to the bellman,
offering half the cheese to the finder for reward.
But the poor man had the dark night round him
coming home, and no great welcome when he got
there, for he had neither the cheese nor its value
no more than his brother.

The four brothers cared for no one's company
but their own, and they all lived together. But
a neighbour who had a few marriageable daughters
said so much about what a shame it was for none
of them to have a wife, that a match was made
up between the eldest and the neighbour's eldest
daughter, and a new house was built for the
couple at the end of the big bawn. The evening
before the wedding, says the bridegroom: " I'm
rather afraid of this change. I've heard of women
tyrannizing over their husbands, and beating them
within an inch of their lives, and if she took a
fancy to throunce me in the night, you wouldn't
hear me from the new house." That speech
frightened the whole family. " Ah!" says the second
eldest, " let it be put in the marriage articles that
there shan't be a stick kept in the house thicker
than your little finger. She can't kill you with
that, anyway." Well, that gave them all great
comfort, till a *gomula* of a servant-boy put in his
word. " Oh, faith, if she's inclined for battle it's
not the little kippeen she'll take to, while she has
the tongs at hand." All were thrown into a
quandary again, but the boy soon gave them
relief. " I'll tell you what we'll do. When the new

102

mistress, God bless her, goes to whack the young master, let him bawl out like a man. The boy will hear him from the stable loft, he'll bawl out, and the thresher will hear him from his shass in the barn. And I'll hear the thresher from the settle-bed in the kitchen. The old mistress'll hear me, and all the house'll hear her." They all clapped their hands for joy, and the marriage didn't frighten anyone. The stable boy, and the thresher, and the boy in the settle said they didn't close an eye for a whole week after the marriage, for fear of an attack on the master. I don't believe them. No one stayed awake after that, and the bridegroom might be killed for anything they done to hinder it.

At last all were married to the other sisters, but the dickens a foot farther than the four corners of the big bawn they'd separate from one another.

They were all conversing one day in the bawn, and one of them made a remark that put them all into a great fright. " Aren't there four brothers of us altogether?" says he. " To be sure," says one, and " To be sure," says another, and " To be sure," says the last. " Well," says he, " I'm after counting, and I can't make out one more than three." "And neither can I," says one, and " Neither can I," says another, and " Neither can I," says the last. " Some one must be dead or gone away." Well, they were all in a great fright, I can tell you, for a while. At last says the one who spoke first, " Let every one go and sit on a ridge of his house, and I'll soon see who is missing." Well, they done so, and then the poor fellow that stayed to count, after looking all round, cried out, " Oh, murdher, murdher! there's no one on my own house. It's myself that's missing." That's all I ever heard of the wise men of Gotham, and I'm sure it's no great loss.

The Greek Princess and the Young Gardener

There was once a king, but I didn't hear what country he was over, and he had one very beautiful daughter. Well, he was getting old and sickly, and the doctors found out that the finest medicine in the world for him was the apples of a tree that grew in the orchard just under his window. So you may be sure he had the tree well-minded, and used to get the apples counted from the time they were the size of small marbles. One harvest, just as they were beginning to turn ripe, the king was awoke one night by the flapping of wings outside in the orchard, and when he looked out, what did he see but a bird among the branches of his tree. Its feathers were so bright they made a light all round them, and the minute it saw the old sickly king in his night-cap and night-shirt it picked off an apple, and flew away. " Oh, tattheration to that thief of a gardener!" says he, " this is a nice way he's watching my precious fruit."

He didn't sleep a wink the rest of the night; and as soon as anyone was stirring in the palace, he sent for the gardener, and abused him for his neglect. " Please, your majesty," says he, " not

104

another apple you shall lose. My three sons are the best shots at the bow-arra in the kingdom, and they and myself will watch in turn every night."

When the night came, the gardener's eldest son took his post in the garden with his bow strung and his arrow between his fingers, and watched, and watched. But at the dead hour the king, who was wide awake, heard the flapping of wings, and ran to the window. There was the bright bird in the tree, and the boy fast asleep, sitting with his back to the wall and his bow on his lap. " Rise, you lazy thief!" says the king. " There's the bird again, tattheration to her!" Up jumped the poor fellow; but while he was fumbling with the arrow and the string, away was the bird with the nicest apple on the tree. Well, to be sure, how the king fumed and fretted, and how he abused the gardener and the boy, and what a twenty-four hours he spent till midnight came again!

He had his eye this time on the second son of the gardener; but though he was up and lively enough when the clock began to strike twelve, it wasn't done with the last bang when he saw him stretched like one dead on the long grass, and saw the bright bird again, and heard the flap of her wings, and saw her carry away the third apple. The poor fellow woke with the roar the king let at him, and even was time enough to let fly an arrow after the bird. He did not hit her, you may depend; and though the king was mad enough, he saw the poor fellows were under pishrogues, and could not help it.

Well, he had some hopes out of the youngest, for he was a brave active young fellow that had

105

everybody's good word. There he was ready, and there was the king watching him and talking to him at the first stroke of twelve. At the last clang, the brightness coming before the bird lighted up the wall and the trees, and the rushing of the wings was heard as it flew into the branches; but at the same instant the crack of the arrow on her side might be heard a quarter of a mile off. Down came the arrow and a large feather was thrown along with it, and away was the bird with a screech that was enough to break the drum of your ear. She hadn't time to carry off an apple; and bedad, when the feather was thrown into the king's room it was heavier than lead, and turned out to be the finest beaten gold.

Well, there was great cooramuch made about the youngest boy next day, and he watched night after night for a week but not a smite of a bird or bird's feather was to be seen, and then the king told him to go home and sleep. Everyone admired the beauty of the gold feather beyond anything, but the king was fairly bewitched. He was turning it round and round, and rubbing it again' his forehead and his nose the live-long day; and at last he proclaimed that he'd give his daughter and half his kingdom to whoever would bring him the bird with the gold feathers, dead or alive.

The gardener's eldest son had great consate out of himself and away he set to try for the bird. In the afternoon he sat down under a tree to rest himself, and eat a bit of bread and cold meat that he had in his wallet, when up comes as fine alook-ing fox as you'd see in the burrow of Munfin. "Musha, sir," says he, "would you spare a bit of that meat to a poor body that's hungry?" " Well," says the other, " you must have the divel's own assurance, you common robber, to ask me such a question. Here's the answer," and he let fly at the moddhereen rua. The arrow scraped from his side up over his back, as if he was made of hammered iron, and stuck in a tree a couple of perches off. " Foul play," says the fox, " but I respect your young brother and will give you a bit of advice. At nightfall you'll come into a village. One side of the street you'll see a large room lighted up, and filled with young men and women dancing and drinking. The other side you'll see a house with no light, only from the fire in the front room, and no one near it but a man and his wife and their child. Take a fool's advice and get lodging there." With that he curled his tail over his crupper and trotted off.

The boy found things as the fox said, but begonies he chose the dancing and drinking, and there we'll leave him. In a week's time, when they got tired at home waiting for him, the second son said he'd try his fortune, and off he set. He was just as ill-natured and foolish as his brother, and the same thing happened to him. Well, when a week was over, away went the youngest of all, and as sure as the hearth-money, he sat under the same tree and pulled out his bread and meat, and the same fox came up and saluted him. Well, the young fellow shared his dinner with the moddhereen and he wasn't long beating about the bush, but told the other he knew all about the business. " I'll help you," says he, " if I find you're biddable. So just at nightfall you'll come into a village. . . .

107

Good-bye till to-morrow." It was just as the fox said, but the boy took care not to go near dancer, drinker, fiddler or piper. He got welcome in the quiet house to supper and bed, and was on his journey next morning before the sun was the height of the trees.

He wasn't gone a quarter of a mile when he saw the fox coming out of a wood that was by the roadside. " Good morrow, fox," says one. " Good morrow, sir," says the other. " Have you any notion how far you have to travel till you find the golden bird?" " Dickens a notion have I—how could I?" " Well, I have. She's in the King of Spain's palace, and that's a good two hundred miles off." " Oh, dear! we'll be a week going." " No, we won't. Sit down on my tail, and we'll soon make the road short." " Tail indeed! That 'ud be the droll saddle, my poor moddhereen." " Do as I tell you, or I'll leave you to yourself." Well, rather than vex him he sat down on the tail that was spread out level like a wing, and away they went like thought. They overtook the wind that was before them, and the wind that came after didn't overtake them. In the afternoon, they stopped in a wood near the King of Spain's palace, and there they stayed till nightfall.

" Now," says the fox, " I'll go before you to make the minds of the guards easy, and you'll have nothing to do but go from one lighted hall to another lighted hall till you find the golden bird in the last. If you have a head on you, you'll bring himself and his cage outside the door, and no one then can lay hands on him or you. If you haven't a head I can't help you, nor no one else." So he. went over to the gates.

In a quarter of an hour the boy followed, and in the first hall he passed he saw a score of armed guards standing upright, but all dead asleep. In the next he saw a dozen, and in the next half a dozen, and in the next three, and in the room beyond that there was no guard at all, nor lamp, nor candle, but it was as bright as day; for there was the golden bird in a common wood and wire cage, and on the table were the three apples turned into solid gold.

On the same table was the most lovely golden cage eye ever beheld, and it entered the boy's head that it would be a thousand pities not to put the precious bird into it, the common cage was so un-fit for him. Maybe he thought of the money it was worth; anyhow he made the exchange, and he had good reason to be sorry for it. The instant the shoulder of the bird's wing touched the golden wires, he let such a squawk out of him as was enough to break all the panes of glass in the win-dows, and at the same minute the three men, and the half dozen, and the dozen, and the score men, woke up and clattered their swords and spears, and surrounded the poor boy, and jibed, and cursed, and swore at him till he didn't know whether it's his foot or head he was standing on. They called the king and told him what happened, and he put on a very grim face. " It's on a gibbet you ought to be this moment," says he, " but I'll give you a chance of your life, and of the golden bird, too. I lay you under prohibitions, and restrictions, and death, and destruction, to go and bring me the

109

King of Morocco's bay filly that outruns the wind, and leaps over the wall of castle-bawns. When you fetch her into the bawn of this palace, you must get the golden bird and liberty to go where you please."

Out passed the boy, very down-hearted, but as he went along, who should come out of a brake but the fox again!

"Ah, my friend," says he, "I was right when I suspected you hadn't a head on you; but I won't rub your hair again' the grain. Get on my tail again and when we come to the King of Morocco's palace we'll see what we can do." So away they went like thought. The wind, &c. &c. &c.

Well, the nightfall came on them in a wood near the palace, and says the fox: "I'll go and make things easy for you at the stables, and when you are leading out the filly, don't let her touch the door, nor door-posts, nor anything but the ground, and that with her hoofs; and if you haven't a head on you once you are in the stable, you'll be worse off than before."

So the boy delayed for a quarter of an hour, and then he went into the big bawn of the palace. There were two rows of armed men reaching from the gate to the stable, and every man was in the depth of deep sleep, and through them went the boy till he got into the stable. There was the filly, as handsome a beast as ever stretched leg, and there was one stable boy with a currycomb in his hand, and another with a bridle, and another with a sieve of oats, and another with an armful of hay, and all as if they were cut out of stone. The filly was the only live thing in the place except himself.

110

She had a common wood and leather saddle on her back, but a golden saddle with the nicest work on it was hung from the post, and he thought it the greatest pity not to put it in place of the other. Well, I believe there was some pishrogues over it for a saddle; anyhow he took off the other, and put the gold one in its place.

Out came a squeal from the filly's throat when she felt the strange article, that might be heard from Tombrick to Bunclody, and all as ready were the armed men and the stable boys to run and surround the omadhan of a boy, and the King of Morocco was soon there along with the rest, with a face on him as black as the sole of your foot. After he stood enjoying the abuse the poor boy got from everybody for some time, he says to him, " You deserve high hanging for your impedence, but I'll give you a chance for your life and your filly too. I lay on you all sorts of prohibitions, and restrictions, and death, and destruction to go bring me Princess Golden Locks, the King of Greek's daughter. When you deliver her into my hand, you may have the ' daughter of the wind ' and welcome. Come in and take your supper and your rest, and be off at the flight of night."

The poor boy was down in the mouth, you may suppose, as he was walking away next morning, and very much ashamed when the fox looked up in his face after coming out of the wood. " What a thing it is," says he, " not to have a head when a body wants it worse; and here we have a fine long journey before us to the king of Greek's palace. The worse luck now, the same always. Here, get on my tail, and we'll be making the road shorter."

111

So he sat on the fox's tail, and swift as thought they went. The wind that, &c. &c. &c., and in the evening they were eating their bread and cold meat in the wood near the castle.

"Now," says the fox, when they were done, "I'll go before you to make things easy. Follow me in a quarter of an hour. Don't let Princess Golden Locks touch the jambs of the doors with her hands, or hair, or clothes, and if you're asked any favour, mind how you answer. Once she's outside the door, no one can take her from you." Into the palace walked the boy at the proper time, and there were the score, the dozen, and the half dozen, and the three guards all standing up or leaning on their arms, and all dead asleep, and in the farthest room of all was the Princess Golden Locks, as lovely as Venus herself. She was asleep in one chair, and her father, the King of Greek, in another. He stood before her ever so long, with the love sinking deeper into his heart every minute, till at last he went down on one knee, and took her darling white hand in his hand, and kissed it.

When she opened her eyes, she was a little frightened, but I believe not very angry, for the boy, as I call him, was a fine handsome young fellow, and all the respect and love that ever you could think of was in his face. She asked him what he wanted, and he stammered, and blushed, and began his story six times, before she understood it. "And would you give me up to that ugly black King of Morocco?" says she. "I am obliged to do so," says he, "by prohibitions, and restrictions, and death, and destruction, but I'll have his life and free you, or lose my own. If I can't get you for

my wife, my days on the earth will be short."
" Well," says she, " let me take leave of my father
at any rate." "Ah, I can't do that," says he,
" or they'd all waken, and myself would be put
to death, or sent to some task worse than any I got
yet." But she asked leave at any rate to kiss the
old man—that wouldn't waken him, and then
she'd go. How could he refuse her, and his heart
tied up in every curl of her hair? But, bedad, the
moment her lips touched her father's, he let a cry,
and every one of the score, the dozen . . . guards
woke up, and clashed their arms, and were going
to make gibbets of the foolish boy.

But the king ordered them to hold their hands,
till he'd be told of what it was all about, and
when he heard the boy's story he gave him a
chance for his life. " There is," says he, " a great
heap of clay in front of the palace, that won't let
the sun shine on the walls in the middle of summer.
Every one that ever worked at it found two shovel-
fuls added to it for every one they threw away.
Remove it and I'll let my daughter go with you.
If you're the man I suspect you to be, I think she'll
be in no danger of being wife to that yellow
Mollott."

Early next morning was the boy tackled to his
work, and for every shovelful he flung away two
came back on him, and at last he could hardly get
out of the heap that gathered round him. Well,
the poor fellow scrambled out some way, and sat
down on a sod, and he'd have cried only for the
shame of it. He began at it in ever so many places,
and one was still worse than the other, and in the
heel of the evening, when he was sitting with his

head between his hands, who should be standing before him but the fox. "Well, my poor fellow," says he, "you're low enough. Go in: I won't say anything to add to your trouble. Take your supper and your rest: to-morrow will be a new day."

"How is the work going off," says the king when they were at supper. "Faith, your Majesty," says the poor boy, "it's not going off, but coming on it is. I suppose you'll have the trouble of digging me out at sunset to-morrow, and waking me." "I hope not," says the princess with a smile on her kind face, and the boy was as happy as anything the rest of the evening.

He was wakened up next morning with voices shouting, and bugles blowing, and drums beating, and such a hullibulloo he never heard in his life before. He ran out to see what was the matter, and there, where the heap of clay was the evening before, were soldiers, and servants, and lords, and ladies, dancing like mad for joy that it was gone. "Ah, my poor fox!" says he to himself, "this is your work." Well, there was little delay about his return. The King was going to send a great retinue with the princess and himself, but he wouldn't let him take the trouble. "I have a friend," says he, "that will bring us both to the King of Morocco's palace in a day, d— fly away with him!"

There was great crying when she was parting from her father. "Ah!" says he, "what a lonesome life I'll have now! Your poor brother in the power of that wicked witch, and kept away from us, and now you taken from me in my old age!" Well, while they both were walking on through the wood and he telling her how much he loved her, out

114

walked the fox from behind a brake, and in a short time he and she were sitting on the brush and holding one another fast for fear of slipping off, and away they went like thought. The wind, &c. &c., and in the evening he and she were in the big bawn of the King of Morocco's castle.

" Well," says he to the boy, " you done your duty well; bring out the bay filly. I'd give the full of the bawn of such fillies if I had them, for this handsome princess. Get on your steed, and here is a good purse of guineas for the road." " Thank you," says he. " I suppose you'll let me shake hands with the princess before I start." " Yes, indeed, and welcome." Well, he was some little time about the hand-shaking, and before it was over he had her fixed snug behind him; and while you could count three, he and she and the filly were through all the guards and a hundred perches away. On they went, and next morning they were in the wood near the King of Spain's palace, and there was the fox before them. " Leave your princess here with me," says he, and go get the golden bird and the three apples. If you don't bring us back the filly along with the bird I must carry you both home myself."

Well, when the King of Spain saw the boy and the filly in the bawn he made the golden bird, and the golden cage, and the golden apples be brought out and handed to him, and was very thankful and very glad of his prize. But the boy could not part with the nice beast without petting it and rubbing it, and while no one was expecting such a thing, he was up on its back and through the guards and a hundred perches away, and he wasn't long till he came where he left his princess and the fox.

They hurried away till they were safe out of the King of Spain's land, and then they went on easier; and if I was to tell you all the loving things they said to one another, the story wouldn't be over till morning. When they were passing the village of the dance house they found his two brothers begging, and they brought them along. When they came to where the fox appeared first, he begged the young man to cut off his head and his tail. He would not do it for him; he shivered at the thought, but the eldest brother was ready enough. The head and tail vanished with the blows, and the body changed into the finest young man you could see, and who was he but the princess's brother that was bewitched. Whatever joy they had before, they had twice as much now, and when they arrived at the palace bonfires were set blazing, oxen roasting and puncheons of wine put out in the lawn. The young Prince of Greek was married to the King's daughter, and the prince's sister to the gardener's son. He and she went a shorter way back to her father's house with many attendants, and the King was so glad of the golden bird and the golden apples that he sent a wagon full of gold and a wagon full of silver along with them.

Shan an Omadhan and his Master

A poor woman had three sons. The eldest and second eldest were cunning fellows, but they called the youngest Shan an Omadhan, because they thought he was no better than a simpleton. The eldest got tired of staying at home, and said he'd go look for service. He stayed away a whole year, and then came back one day, dragging one foot after the other, and a poor wizened face on him, and he as cross as two sticks. When he was rested and got something to eat, he told them how he got service with the Bodach Liath of Tuaim an Drochaigh (Gray Churl of the Townland of Mischance), and that the agreement was, whoever would first say he was sorry for his bargain, should get an inch wide of the skin of his back, from shoulder to hip, taken off. If it was the master, he should also pay double wages; if it was the servant he should get no wages at all. "But the thief," says he, " gave me so little to eat, and kept me so hard at work, that flesh and blood couldn't stand it; and when he asked me once, when I was in a passion, if I was sorry for my bargain, I was mad enough to say I was and here I am disabled for life."

Vexed enough were the poor mother and brothers; and the second eldest said on the spot he'd go and take service with the Gray Churl, and punish him by all the annoyance he'd give him till he'd make him say he was sorry for his agreement. " Oh, won't I be glad to see the skin coming off the old villain's back!" said he. All they could say had no effect: he started off for the Townland of Mischance, and in a twelvemonth he was back just as miserable and helpless as his brother.

All the poor mother could say didn't prevent Shan an Omadhan from starting to see if he was

117

able to regulate the Bodach Liath. He agreed with him for a year for twenty pounds, and the terms were the same.

"Now, Shan," said the Bodach Liath, "if you refuse to do anything you are able to do, you must lose a month's wages." "I'm satisfied," said Shan, "and if you stop me from doing a thing after telling me to do it, you are to give me an additional month's wages." "I am satisfied," said the master.

The first day that Shan served he was fed very poorly, and was worked to the saddleskirts. Next day he came in just before the dinner was sent up to the parlour. They were taking the goose off the spit, but well becomes Shan, he whips a knife off the dresser, and cuts off one side of the breast, one leg and thigh, and one wing, and fell to. In came the master, and began to abuse him for his assurance. "Oh, you know, master, you're to feed me, and wherever the goose goes won't have to be filled again till supper. Are you sorry for our agreement?" The master was going to cry out he was, but he bethought himself in time. "Oh, no, not at all," said he. "That's well," said Shan.

Next day Jack was to go clamp turf on the bog. They weren't sorry to have him away from the kitchen at dinner time. He didn't find his breakfast very heavy on his stomach; so he said to the mistress, "I think, Ma'am, it will be better for me to get my dinner now, and not lose time coming home from the bog." "That's true, Shan," said she. So she brought out a good cake, and a print of butter, and a bottle of milk, thinking he'd take them away to the bog. But Shan kept his

118

seat, and never drew rein till bread, butter, and milk went down the red lane. " Now, mistress," said he, " I'll be earlier at my work to-morrow if I sleep comfortably on the sheltery side of a clamp on dry grass, and not be coming here and going back. So you may as well give me my supper, and be done with the day's trouble." She gave him that, thinking he'd take it to the bog; but he fell to on the spot, and did not leave a scrap to tell tales on him; and the mistress was a little astonished.

He called to speak to the master in the haggard, and said he, " What are servants asked to do in this country after aten their supper?" " Nothing at all, but go to bed." " Oh, very well, sir." He went up on the stable-loft, stripped, and lay down, and someone that saw him told the master. He came up. " Shan, you anointed 'sthronshuch, what do you mean?" " To go to sleep, master. The mistress, God bless her, is after giving me my breakfast, dinner and supper, and yourself told me that bed was the next thing. Do you blame me, sir?" " Yes, you rascal, I do." " Hand me one pound thirteen and fourpence, if you please, sir." " One divel and thirteen imps, you tinker! what for?" " Oh, I see, you've forgot your bargain. Are you sorry for it?" " Oh, ya—no, I mean, I'll give you the money after your nap."

Next morning early, Jack asked how he'd be employed that day. " You are to be holding the plough in that fallow, outside the paddock." The master went over about nine o'clock to see what kind of a ploughman was Shan, and what did he see but the little boy driving the bastes, and the sock and coulter of the plough skimming along the sod, and Shan pulling ding-dong again' the horses. "What are you doing, you conthrary thief?" said the master. "An' ain't I strivin' to hold this divel of a plough, as you told me; but that rascal of a boy keeps whipping on the bastes in spite of all I say; will you speak to him?" "No, but I'll speak to you. Didn't you know, you bosthoon, that when I said 'holding the plough', I meant reddening the ground?" "Faith an' if you did, I wish you had said so. Do you blame me for what I have done?" The master caught himself in time, but he was so stomached, he said nothing. "Go on and redden the ground now, you knave, as other ploughmen do." "An' are you sorry for our agreement?" "Oh, no, not at all, mauya." Shan ploughed away like a good workman all the rest of the day.

In a day or two the master bade him go and mind the cows in a field that had half of it under young corn. "Be sure, particularly," said he, "to keep Browney from the wheat; while she's out of mischief there's no fear of the rest." About noon, he went to see how Shan was doing his duty, and what did he find but Jack asleep with his face to the sod, Browney grazing near a thorn-tree, one end of a long rope round her horns, and the other end round the tree, and the rest of the beasts all trampling and eating the green wheat. Down came the switch on Shan. "Shan, you vagabone, do you see what the cows are at?" "And do you blame me, master?" "To be sure, you lazy slug-gard, I do." "Hand me out one pound thirteen and fourpence, master. You said if I only kept Browney out of mischief, the rest would do no harm. There she is as harmless as a lamb. Are you sorry for hiring me, master?" "To be—that is, not at all. I'll give you your money when you go to dinner. Now, understand me; don't let a cow go out of the field nor into the wheat the rest of the day." "Never fear, master!" and neither did he. But the bodach would rather than a great deal he had not hired him.

The next day three heifers were missing, and the master bade Jack go in search of them. "Where will I look for them?" said Shan. "Oh, every place likely and unlikely for them all to be in." The bodach was getting very exact in his words. When he was coming into the bawn at dinner-time, what work did he find Jack at but pulling armfuls of the thatch off the roof, and peeping into the holes he was making. "What are you doing there, you rascal?" "Sure, I'm looking for the heifers, poor things!" "What would bring them there?" "I don't think anything could bring them in it; but I looked first into the likely places, that is, the cow-houses, and the pastures, and the fields next 'em, and now I'm looking in the un-likeliest places I can think of. Maybe it's not pleasing to you, it is." "And to be sure it isn't pleasing to me, you aggravating *googein*!" "Please, sir, hand me one pound thirteen and fourpence before you sit down to your dinner. I'm afraid it's sorrow that's on you for hiring me at all." "May the div—oh no; I'm not sorry. Will you begin, if you please, and put in the thatch again, just as if you were doing it for your mother's cabin?" "Oh, faith, I will, sir, with a heart and a half"; and by the time the farmer

121

came out from his dinner, Shan had the roof better than it was before, for he made the boy give him new straw.

Says the master when he came out, " Go, Shan, and look for the heifers and bring them home." " And where will I look for 'em?" " Go and search for them as if they were your own." The heifers were all in the paddock before sunset.

Next morning, says the bodach, " Jack, the path across the bog to the pasture is very bad; the sheep does be sinking in it every step; go and make it a good path with the sheep's feet." About an hour after he came to the edge of the bog, and what did he find Shan at but sharpening a carving knife, and the sheep standing or gazing round. " Is this the way you are mending the path, Shan?" said he. " Everything must have a beginning, master," said Shan, " and a thing well begun is half done. I am sharpening the knife, and I'll have the feet off every sheep in the flock while you'd be blessing yourself." " Feet off my sheep, you anointed rogue! And what would you be taking their feet off for?" " An' sure to mend the path as you told me. Says you, ' Shan, *dean staidhear,* &c., make a path with the feet of the sheep '." " Oh, you fool, I meant make good the path for the sheep's feet." " It's a pity you didn't say so, master. Hand me out one pound thirteen and fourpence if you don't like me to finish my job." " Divel do you good with your one pound thirteen and fourpence!" " It's better pray than curse, master. Maybe you're sorry for your bargain?" " And to be sure I am—not yet, any way."

The next night the bodach was going to a wedding, and says he to Jack before he set out : " I'll leave at midnight and I wish you to come and be with me home, for fear I might be overtaken with the drink. If you're there before, you may throw a sheep's eye at me, and I'll be sure to see that they'll give you something for yourself."

About eleven o'clock while the bodach was in great spirits, he felt something clammy hit him on the cheek. It fell beside his tumbler, and what was it but the eye of a sheep, and a very ugly looking article it was. Well, he couldn't imagine who threw it at him, or why it was thrown at him. After a little he got a blow on the other cheek, and still it was by another sheep's eye. Well, he was very vexed, but he thought better to say nothing. In two minutes more, when he was opening his mouth to take a sup, another sheep's eye was slapped into it. He sputtered it out, and cried, " Man o' the house, isn't it a great shame for you to have any one in the room that would do such a nasty thing?" " Master," says Shan, " don't blame the honest man. Sure, it's only myself that was throwin' them sheep's eyes at you, to remind you I was here, and that I wanted to drink the bride and bridegroom's health. You know yourself bade me." " I know you are a great rascal; and where did you get the eyes?" " An' where would I get 'em but in the heads of your own sheep? Would you have me meddle with the bastes of any neighbour, who might put me in the Stone Jug for it?" " *Mo chuma* that ever I had the bad luck to meet with you."

" You're all witness," says Jack, " that my master says he is sorry for having met with me.

123

My time is up. Master, hand me over double wages, and come into the next room and lay yourself out like a man that has some decency in him till I take a strip of skin an inch broad from your shoulder to your hip." Every one shouted out against that; but, says Shan, "You didn't hinder him when he took the same strips from the backs of my two brothers, and sent them home in that state, and penniless, to their poor mother." When the company heard the rights of the business, they were only too eager to see the job done. The bodach bawled and roared, but there was no help at hand. He was stripped to his hips, and laid on the floor in the next room, and Jack had the carving knife in his hand ready to begin. "Now, you cruel old villain," said he, giving the knife a couple of scrapes along the floor, "I'll make you an offer. Give me, along with my double wages, two hundred pounds to support my poor brothers, and I'll do without the strap." "No!" said he, "I'd let you skin me from head to foot first." "Here goes, then," said Shan with a grin, but the first little scar he gave, bodach roared out, "Stop your hand; I'll give the money."

"Now, neighbours," said Shan, "you mustn't think worse of me than I deserve. I wouldn't have the heart to take an eye out of a rat itself; I got half a dozen of them from the butcher, and only used three of them."

So all came again into the other room, and Shan was made sit down, and everybody drank his health, and he drank everybody's health at one offer. And six stout fellows saw himself and the bodach home, and waited in the parlour while he went up and

124

brought down the two hundred pounds and double wages for Shan himself. When he got home, he brought the summer along with him to the poor mother and the disabled brothers; and he was no more Shan an Omadhan in the people's mouths but Shan a'Ruisgeach, " Jack the Skinner ".

The Wonderful Cake

A mouse, a rat, and a little red hen once lived together in the same cabin, and one day the little red hen said, " Let us bake a cake and have a feast." " Let us," says the mouse; and " let us," says the rat. " Who'll go get the wheat ground?" says the hen. " I won't," says the mouse. " I won't," says the rat. " I will myself," says the little red hen. " Who'll make the cake?" " I won't," says the mouse. " I won't," says the rat. " I will myself," says the little red hen. " Who'll eat the cake?" " I will," says the mouse. " I will," says the rat. " Dickens a bit you shall," says the little red hen. Well, while the hen was putting over her hand to it, *magh go bragh* with it out of the door, and after it with the three housekeepers.

When it was running away, it went by a barn full of thrashers and they asked it where it was running. " Oh," says it, " I'm running away from the mouse, the rat, and the little red hen, and from you, too, if I can." So they piked away after it with

125

their flails, and it run and it run till it came to a ditch full of ditchers, and they asked it where it was running. " Oh, I'm running away from the mouse, the rat, and the little red hen, and from a barn full of thrashers, and from you, too, if I can." Well, they all ran after it along with the rest till it came to a well full of washers, and they asked the same question, and it returned the same answer, and after it they went. At last it came to a ford where it met with a fox, who asked where it was running. " Oh, I'm running away from the mouse, the rat, the little red hen, from a barn full of thrashers, a well full of washers, a crumply-horned cow, and saddled-backed sow, and from you, too, if I can." " But you can't cross the ford," says the fox. " What'll you give me?" says the fox. " A kiss at Christmas, and an egg at Easter," says the cake. " Very well," says the fox. " Up with you."

So he sat on his currabingo with his nose in the air, and the cake got up by his tail till it sat on his crupper. " Now, over with you," says the cake. " You're not high enough." Then it scrambled up on his shoulder. " Up higher still," says he. " You wouldn't be safe there." " Am I right now?" says the cake, when it was on his head. " Not quite," says the fox. " You'll be safer on the ridge pole of my nose." " Well," says the cake, " I think I can go no further." " Oh, yes," says he, and he shot it up in the air, caught it in his mouth, and sent it down the red lane.

GLOSSARY

For the benefit of the foreign reader this list of Irish words (or words derived from the Irish) is appended. Patrick Kennedy's spelling has been retained in the text; though not always correct it seems to be essential to the atmosphere of the narrative. The correct Irish spelling is given in brackets.

banacht lath (*beannacht leat*)—blessing to you.
bodach—an Irish term of great contempt.
Bodach Liath of Tuaim an Drocháidh (*Bodach Liath Tuaim an Drocháidh*)—Grey Churl in the Townland of Mischance.
bohyeen (*bóithrín*) boreen—road.
booltheen (*buailthín*)—the striking staff of a flail.
brishe derives from Irish *briseadh* (breaking).
bresna (*brosna*)—kindling.
Ceann Dhu (*ceann dubh*)—black head—a term of endearment.
Chloive Solais (*claíomh solais*)—sword of light.
colliach (*cailleach*)—old woman, hag.
colliach Cushmor (*cailleach cosmhór*)—big-footed old woman.
Colliach Cromanmor (*cailleach chromán mór*)—big-hipped old woman.
Cooramuch (*cúramach*)—careful, or from Irish *Cúramacht* (carefulness).
Cuileach dhu (*coileach dubh*)—black cock.
currahingo (*corrabionga*)—haunches.
dean staidhear (*déan staidéar*)—pull yourself together.
gaachy (*geatsí*)—cutting gaachy, i.e., showing off.
geochach (*geocach*)—vagrant, mummer.
Gilla na Chreck an Gour (*Giolla an Chraicinn Gabhair*)—the fellow in the goatskin.
giolla—Irish (*giolla*)—retainer.

googein (*guaigín*)—fidgety, unsteady person.

gomula (*gamallach* or *gamalóg*)—fool.

gorsoon (*garsún*)—boy.

Lunacy Day (*Lá Lúnasa*)—the day of the Lug-festival (pagan harvest festival held on dates ranging from July 24 to early in August).

Magh go bragh with themselves (*amach go breá leo*)—out they went.

meentrach (*muintreach*)—friendly, neighbourly.

mishe (*mise*)—myself.

mile mollacht (*míle mallacht*)—thousand curses.

mo chuma (*mo chumha*)—my sorrow.

moddhera rua (*madra rua*)—fox.

an Omadhan (*an t-amadán*)—the fool.

onshuch (*óinseach*)—a female fool.

rinka-fadha (*rince fada*)—long dance; a folk dance.

sha go deine (*sea go deimhin*)—yes, certainly.

shass (*seas*)—bench in a hayrick, sheaves ready for threshing.

shron mor rua (*srón mhór rua*)—big red nose.

shuler (*siúlóir*)—traveller or tramp.

skian (*scian*)—knife.

sleeveen (*slíbhín*)—a mean, scheming person.

on the sthra—idling; cf. Irish (*sraith*)—swathe of hay.

Tather Jack Walsh—an Irish folk-dance tune, a double jig, extremely popular, originally *an t-athair Jack Breatnach*.

thraneen (*tráithnín*)—stem or stalk.

thuckeen (*tuicín*)—young girl.

travally—such as travally ruz—there was such an outcry caused (travally cf. French *travail*).

vanitee—cf. Irish (*bean an tí*)—housewife; woman of the house.